D0427131

OBFUSCATION

OBFUSCATION

A USER'S GUIDE
FOR PRIVACY AND PROTEST

Finn Brunton | Helen Nissenbaum

The MIT Press
Cambridge, Massachusetts
London, England

MIT Press books may be purchased at special quantity discounts for business or sales promotional use. For information, email special_sales@mitpress.mit.edu.

Set in PF Din Text Cond Pro by Toppan Best-set Premedia Limited. Printed and bound in the United States of America.

Library of Congress Cataloging-in-Publication Data are available.
ISBN: 978-0-262-02973-5

10 9 8 7 6 5 4 3 2 1

CONTENTS

II UNDERSTANDING OBFUSCATION

ACKNOWLEDGMENTS

This book began with technology—the TrackMeNot project—and we owe our deepest thanks to Daniel Howe, who got it on its feet, and Vincent Toubiana, who joined the effort, expanded its scope, and continues tirelessly to support it and its adopters. Feedback and comments from the community of users and from the privacy community at large, and a joint technical paper with Lakshminarayanan Subramanian (Vincent Toubiana, Lakshminarayanan Subramanian, and Helen Nissenbaum, "TrackMeNot: Enhancing the Privacy of Web Search") have opened our eyes to its potential and limitations. More recently, creating and launching a second system, AdNauseam, with Daniel Howe, in collaboration with the designer Mushon Zer-Aviv, further expanded our perspective on obfuscation and on the need for a deeper, systematic appreciation of what it offers as a method and a strategy.

As we began to work on a general understanding of obfuscation, we were able to explore many of the concepts in a paper published in *First Monday* and a chapter in *Privacy, Due Process and the Computational Turn,* which benefited enormously from review and editorial feedback in those venues.

Obfuscation became a book with the encouragement and thorough advice of the reviewers and of Marguerite Avery, Gita Manaktala, Susan Buckley, Katie Helke, and Paul Bethge at the MIT Press. Our thanks to all of them. Emily Goldsher-Diamond did meticulous work as a research assistant, as well as organizing many other aspects of this project. Work on this book through all its drafts was supported by grants from the National Science Foundation (ITR-0331542: Sensitive Information in a Wired World), from EAGER (CNS-1355398: Values in Design for Future Internet Architecture—Next Phase), from the Air Force Office of Scientific Research (MURI-ONR BAA 07-036: Collaborative Policies and Assured Information Sharing), and from the Intel Science and Technology Center for Social Computing. Support from these grants provided time, technology, and a collegial context for pursuing this project and bringing it to fruition.

Two major events helped shape and refine our thinking about obfuscation. One was the Symposium on Obfuscation (February 15, 2014), jointly organized by New York University's Department of Media, Culture, and Communication and the Information Law Institute and co-sponsored by the Intel Science and Technology Center for Social Computing. For making this event possible, we would like to thank Nicole Arzt, Emily Goldsher-Diamond, Dove Helena Pedlosky, Melissa Lucas-Ludwig, Erica Robles-Anderson, and Jamie Schuler— and, above all, Seda Gürses, who organized, structured, and shaped so much of the day. Every single speaker had a direct effect on our manuscript. The other event was the ongoing conversation of the Privacy Research Group at NYU, at whose weekly seminars we presented several stages of this material. The book would not have this final form without the PRG discussions; our fond thanks to everyone involved.

Other opportunities to present and test aspects of this work have been enormously productive, and our ideas have been greatly improved by the responses of supporters, critics, believers, and skeptics. These opportunities have included a joint MIT Center for Civic Media and Comparative Media Studies Colloquium; The New School for Social Research 2014 Graduate Conference; New Media Salon, Tel Aviv; Communications and Journalism Departmental Seminar, Hebrew University of Jerusalem; IBM R&D Labs, Haifa; Eyebeam Art + Technology Center; HotPETS 2013; Computers, Privacy and Data Protection, Brussels; and the Surveillance Studies Conference, Queens University.

We are deeply grateful for friends and colleagues with whom we could discuss obfuscation as it developed, and who offered feedback, criticism, encouragement, and ideas. In particular we would like to thank Julia Angwin, Solon Barocas, danah boyd, Claudia Diaz, Cynthia Dwork, Cathy Dwyer, Tarleton Gillespie, Mireille Hildebrandt, Ari Juels, Nick Montfort, Deirdre Mulligan, Arvind Narayanan, Martijn van Otterloo, Ira Rubinstein, Ian Spiro, Luke Stark, Katherine Strandburg, Matthew Tierney, Joe Turow, Janet Vertesi, Tal Zarsky, Malte Ziewitz, and Ethan Zuckerman.

Finally, this book would not have been possible without the support of our professional home base, the Department of Media, Culture, and Communication at New York University. Thanks to you all!

OBFUSCATION

INTRODUCTION

We mean to start a revolution with this book. But not a big revolution—at least, not at first. Our revolution does not rely on sweeping reforms, on a comprehensive Year Zero reinvention of society, or on the seamless and perfectly uniform adoption of a new technology. It is built on preexisting components—what a philosopher would call tools ready-to-hand, what an engineer would call commodity hardware—that are available in everyday life, in movies, in software, in murder mysteries, and even in the animal kingdom. Although its lexicon of methods can be, and has been, taken up by tyrants, authoritarians, and secret police, our revolution is especially suited for use by the small players, the humble, the stuck, those not in a position to decline or opt out or exert control over our data emanations. The focus of our limited revolution is on mitigating and defeating present-day digital surveillance. We will add concepts and techniques to the existing and expanding toolkit for evasion, noncompliance, outright refusal, deliberate sabotage, and use according to *our* terms of service. Depending on the adversary, the goals, and the resources, we provide methods for disappearance, for time-wasting and analysis-frustrating, for prankish disobedience, for collective protest, for acts of individual redress both great and small. We draw an outline around a whole domain of both established and emerging instances that share a common approach we can generalize and build into policies, software, and action. This outline is the banner under which our big little revolution rides, and the space it defines is called *obfuscation.*

In a sentence: *Obfuscation is the deliberate addition of ambiguous, confusing, or misleading information to interfere with surveillance and data collection.* It's a simple thing with many different, complex applications and uses. If you are a software developer or designer, obfuscation you build into your software can keep user data safe—even from yourself, or from whoever acquires your startup—while you provide social networking, geolocation, or other services requiring collection and use of personal information. Obfuscation also offers ways for government agencies to accomplish many of the goals of data collection while minimizing the potential misuses. And if you are a person or a group wanting to live in the modern world without being a subject of pervasive digital surveillance (and an object of subsequent analysis), obfuscation is a lexicon of ways to put some sand in the gears, to buy time, and to hide in the crowd of signals. This book provides a starting point.

Our project has tracked interesting similarities across very different domains in which those who are obliged to be visible, readable, or audible have responded by burying salient signals in clouds and layers of misleading signals. Fascinated by the diverse contexts in which actors reach for a strategy of obfuscation, we have presented, in chapters 1 and 2, dozens of detailed instances that share this general, common thread. Those two chapters, which make up part I of the book, provide a guide to the diverse forms and formats that obfuscation has taken and demonstrate how these instances are crafted and implemented to suit their respective goals and adversaries. Whether on a social network, at a poker table, or in the skies during the Second World War, and whether confronting an adversary in the form of a facial-recognition system, the Apartheid government of 1980s South Africa, or an opponent across the table, properly deployed obfuscation can aid in the protection of privacy and in the defeat of data collection, observation, and analysis. The sheer range of situations and uses discussed in chapters 1 and 2 is an inspiration and a spur: What kind of work can obfuscation do for you?

The cases presented in chapter 1 are organized into a narrative that introduces fundamental questions about obfuscation and describes important approaches to it that are then explored and debated in part II of the book. In chapter 2, shorter cases illustrate the range and the variety of obfuscation applications while also reinforcing underlying concepts.

Chapters 3–5 enrich the reader's understanding of obfuscation by considering why obfuscation has a role to play in various forms of privacy work; the ethical, social, and political problems raised by using obfuscatory tactics; and ways of assessing whether obfuscation works, or can work, in particular scenarios. Assessing whether an obfuscation approach works entails understanding what makes obfuscation distinct from other tools and understanding its particular weaknesses and strengths. The titles of chapters 3–5 are framed as questions.

The first question, asked in chapter 3, is "Why is obfuscation necessary?" In answering that question, we explain how the challenges of present-day digital privacy can be met by obfuscation's utility. We point out how obfuscation may serve to counteract *information asymmetry,* which occurs when data about us are collected in circumstances we may not understand, for purposes we may not understand, and are used in ways we may not understand. Our data will be shared, bought, sold, managed, analyzed, and applied, all of which will have consequences for our lives. Will you get a loan, or an apartment, for which you applied? How much of an insurance risk or a credit risk are you? What guides the advertising you receive? How do so many companies and services know that you're pregnant, or struggling with an addiction, or planning to change jobs? Why do different cohorts, different populations, and different neighborhoods receive different allocations of resources? Are you going to be, as the sinister phrase of our current moment of data-driven antiterrorism has it, "on a list"? Even innocuous or seemingly benign work in this domain has consequences worth considering. Obfuscation has a role to play, not as a *replacement* for governance, business conduct, or technological interventions, or as a one-size-fits-all solution (again, it's a deliberately small, distributed revolution), but as a tool that fits into the larger network of privacy practices. In particular, it's a tool particularly well suited to the category of people without access to other modes of recourse, whether at a particular moment or in general—people who, as it happens, may be unable to deploy optimally configured privacy-protection tools because they are on the weak side of a particular information-power relationship.

Similarly, context shapes the ethical and political questions around obfuscation. Obfuscation's use in multiple domains, from social policy to social networks to personal activity, raises serious concerns. In chapter 4, we ask "Is obfuscation justified?" Aren't we encouraging people to lie, to be willfully inaccurate, or to "pollute" with potentially dangerous noise databases that have commercial and civic applications? Aren't obfuscators who use commercial services free riding on the good will of honest users who are paying for targeted advertising (and the services) by making data about themselves available? And if these practices become widespread, aren't we going to be collectively wasting processing power and bandwidth? In chapter 4 we address these challenges and describe the moral and political calculus according to which particular instances of obfuscation may be evaluated and found to be acceptable or unacceptable.

What obfuscation can and can't accomplish is the focus of chapter 5. In comparison with cryptography, obfuscation may be seen contingent, even shaky. With cryptography, precise degrees of security against brute-force attacks can be calculated with reference to such factors as key length, processing power, and time. With obfuscation such precision is rarely possible, because its strength as a practical tool depends on what users *want* to accomplish and on what specific barriers they may face in respective circumstances of use. Yet complexity does not mean chaos, and success still rests on careful attention to systematic interdependencies. In chapter 5 we identify six common goals for an obfuscation project and relate them to design dimensions. The goals include buying some time, providing cover, deniability, evading observation, interfering with profiling, and expressing protest. The aspects of design we identify include whether an obfuscation project is individual or collective, whether it is known or unknown, whether it is selective or general, and whether it is short-term or long-term. For some goals, for instance, obfuscation may not succeed if the adversary knows that it is being employed; for other goals—such as collective protest or interference with probable cause and production of plausible deniability—it is better if the adversary knows that the data have been poisoned. All of this, of course, depends on what resources are available to the adversary—that is, how much time, energy, attention, and money the adversary is willing to spend on identifying and weeding out obfuscating information. The logic of these relationships holds promise because it suggests that we can learn from reasoning about specific cases how to improve obfuscation in relation to its purpose. Will obfuscation work? Yes— but only in context.

Let's begin.

I

An Obfuscation Vocabulary

There are many obfuscation strategies. They are shaped by the user's purposes (which may range from buying a few minutes of time to permanently interfering with a profiling system), by whether the users work alone or in concert, by its target and its beneficiaries, by the nature of the information to be obfuscated, and by other parameters we will discuss in part II. (Parts I and II can be read independently—you are encouraged to skip ahead if you have questions about obfuscation's purposes, about ethical and political quandaries, or about the circumstances that, we argue, make obfuscation a useful addition to the privacy toolkit.) Before we get to that, though, we want you to understand how of the many specific circumstances of obfuscation can be generalized into a *pattern*. We can link together a family of seemingly disparate events under a single heading, revealing their underlying continuities and suggesting how similar methods can be applied to other contexts and other problems. Obfuscation is contingent, shaped by the problems we seek to address and the adversaries we hope to foil or delay, but It Is characterized by a simple underlying circumstance: unable to refuse or deny observation, we create many plausible, ambiguous, and misleading signals within which the information we want to conceal can be lost.

To illustrate obfuscation in the ways that are most salient to its use and development now, and to provide a reference for the rest of the book, we have selected a set of core cases that exemplify how obfuscation works and what it can do. These cases are organized thematically. Though they aren't suited to a simple typology, we have structured them so that the various choices particular to obfuscation should become clear as you read. In addition to these cases, we present a set of brief examples that illustrate some of obfuscation's other applications and some of its more unusual contexts. With these cases and explanations, you will have an index of obfuscation across all the domains in which we have encountered it. Obfuscation—positive and negative, effective and ineffective, targeted and indiscriminate, natural and artificial, analog and digital—appears in many fields and in many forms.

1 CORE CASES

1.1 Chaff: defeating military radar

During the Second World War, a radar operator tracks an airplane over Hamburg, guiding searchlights and anti-aircraft guns in relation to a phosphor dot whose position is updated with each sweep of the antenna. Abruptly, dots that seem to represent airplanes begin to multiply, quickly swamping the display. The actual plane is in there somewhere, impossible to locate owing to the presence of "false echoes."[1]

The plane has released chaff—strips of black paper backed with aluminum foil and cut to half the target radar's wavelength. Thrown out by the pound and then floating down through the air, they fill the radar screen with signals. The chaff has exactly met the conditions of data the radar is configured to look for, and has given it more "planes," scattered all across the sky, than it can handle.

This may well be the purest, simplest example of the obfuscation approach. Because discovery of an actual airplane was inevitable (there wasn't, at the time, a way to make a plane invisible to radar), chaff taxed the time and bandwidth constraints of the discovery system by creating too many potential targets. That the chaff worked only briefly as it fluttered to the ground and was not a permanent solution wasn't relevant under the circumstances. It only had to work well enough and long enough for the plane to get past the range of the radar.

As we will discuss in part II, many forms of obfuscation work best as time-buying "throw-away" moves. They can get you only a few minutes, but sometimes a few minutes is all the time you need.

The example of chaff also helps us to distinguish, at the most basic level, between approaches to obfuscation. Chaff relies on producing echoes—imitations of the real thing—that exploit the limited scope of the observer. (Fred Cohen terms this the "decoy strategy."[2]) As we will see, some forms of obfuscation *generate genuine but misleading signals*—much as you would protect the contents of one vehicle by sending it out accompanied by several other identical vehicles, or defend a particular plane by filling the sky with other planes—whereas other forms *shuffle genuine signals*, mixing data in an effort to make the extraction of patterns more difficult. Because those who scatter chaff have exact knowledge of their adversary, chaff doesn't have to do either of these things.

If the designers of an obfuscation system have specific and detailed knowledge of the limits of the observer, the system they develop has to work for only one wavelength and for only 45 minutes. If the system their adversary uses for observation is more patient, or if it has a more comprehensive set of capacities for observation, they have to make use of their understanding of the adversary's internal agenda—that is, of what useful information the adversary hopes to extract from data obtained through surveillance—and undermine that agenda by manipulating genuine signals.

Before we turn to the manipulation of genuine signals, let's look at a very different example of flooding a channel with echoes.

1.2 Twitter bots: filling a channel with noise

The two examples we are about to discuss are a study in contrasts. Although producing imitations is their mode of obfuscation, they take us from the Second World War to present-day circumstances, and from radar to social networks. They also introduce an important theme.

In chapter 3, we argue that obfuscation is a tool particularly suited to the "weak"—the situationally disadvantaged, those at the wrong end of asymmetrical power relationships. It is a method, after all, that you have reason to adopt if you can't be invisible—if you can't refuse to be tracked or surveilled, if you can't simply opt out or operate within professionally secured networks. This doesn't mean that it isn't also taken up by the powerful. Oppressive or coercive forces usually have better means than obfuscation at their disposal. Sometimes, though, obfuscation becomes useful to powerful actors—as it did in two elections, one in Russia and one in Mexico. Understanding the choices faced by the groups in contention will clarify how obfuscation of this kind can be employed.

During protests over problems that had arisen in the 2011 Russian parliamentary elections, much of the conversation about ballot-box stuffing and other irregularities initially took place on LiveJournal, a blogging platform that had originated in the United States but attained its greatest popularity in Russia—more than half of its user base is Russian.[3] Though LiveJournal is quite popular, its user base is very small relative to those of Facebook's and Google's various social systems; it has fewer than 2 million active accounts.[4] Thus, LiveJournal is comparatively easy for attackers to shut down by means of distributed denial of service (DDoS) attack—that is, by using computers scattered around the world to issue requests for the site in such volume that the servers making the site available are overwhelmed and legitimate users can't access it. Such an attack on LiveJournal, in conjunction with the arrests of activist bloggers at a protest in Moscow, was a straightforward approach to censorship.[5] When and why, then, did obfuscation become necessary?

The conversation about the Russian protest migrated to Twitter, and the powers interested in disrupting it then faced a new challenge. Twitter has an enormous user base, with infrastructure and security expertise to match. It could not be taken down as easily as LiveJournal. Based in the United States, Twitter was in a much better position to resist political manipulation than Live-Journal's parent company. (Although LiveJournal service is provided by a company set up in the U.S. for that purpose, the company that owns it, SUP Media, is based in Moscow.[6]) To block Twitter outright would require direct government intervention. The LiveJournal attack was done independently, by nationalist hackers who may or may not have the approval and assistance of the Putin/Medvedev administration.[7] Parties interested in halting the political conversation on Twitter therefore faced a challenge that will become familiar as we explore obfuscation's uses: time was tight, and traditional mechanisms for action weren't available. A direct technical approach—either blocking Twitter within a country or launching a worldwide denial-of-service attack—wasn't possible, and political and legal angles of attack couldn't be used. Rather than stop a Twitter conversation, then, attackers can overload it with noise.

During the Russian protests, the obfuscation took the form of thousands of Twitter accounts suddenly piping up and users posting tweets using the same hashtags used by the protesters.[8] Hashtags are a mechanism for grouping tweets together; for example, if I add #obfuscation to a tweet, the symbol # turns the word into an active link—clicking it will bring up all other tweets tagged with #obfuscation. Hashtags are useful for organizing the flood of tweets into coherent conversations on specific topics, and #триумфальная (referring to Triumfalnaya, the location of a protest) became one of several tags people could use to vent their anger, express their opinions, and organize further actions. (Hashtags also play a role in how Twitter determines "trending" and significant topics on the site, which can then draw further attention to what is being discussed under that tag—the site's Trending Topics list often draws news coverage.[9])

If you were following #триумфальная, you would have seen tweet after tweet from Russian activists spreading links to news and making plans. But those tweets began to be interspersed with tweets about Russian greatness, or tweets that seemed to consist of noise, gibberish, or random words and phrases. Eventually those tweets dominated the stream for #триумфальная, and those for other topics related to the protests, to such a degree that tweets relevant to the topic were, essentially, lost in the noise, unable to get any attention or to start a coherent exchange with other users. That flood of new tweets came from accounts that had been inactive for much of their existence. Although they had posted very little from the time of their creation until the time of the protests, now each of them was posting dozens of times an hour. Some of the accounts' purported users had mellifluous names, such as imelixyvyq, wyqufahij, and hihexiq; others had more conventional-seeming names, all built on a firstname_lastname model—for example, latifah_xander.[10]

Obviously, these Twitter accounts were "Twitter bots"—programs purporting to be people and generating automatic, targeted messages. Many of the accounts had been created around the same time. In numbers and in frequency, such messages can easily dominate a discussion, effectively ruining the platform for a specific audience through overuse—that is, obfuscating through the production of false, meaningless signals.

The use of Twitter bots is becoming a reliable technique for stifling Twitter discussion. The highly contentious 2012 Mexican elections provide another example of this strategy in practice, and further refined.[11] Protesters opposed to the front-runner, Enrique Peña Nieto, and to the Partido Revolucionario Institucional (PRI), used #marchaAntiEPN as an organizing hashtag for the purposes of aggregating conversation, structuring calls for action, and arranging protest events. Groups wishing to interfere with the protesters' organizing efforts faced challenges similar to those in the Russian case. Rather than thousands of bots, however, hundreds would do—indeed, when this case was investigated by the American Spanish-language TV network Univision, only about thirty such bots were active. Their approach was both to interfere with the work being done to advance #marchaAntiEPN and to overuse that hashtag. Many of the tweets consisted entirely of variants of "#marchaAntiEPN #marchaAntiEPN #marchaAntiEPN #marchaAntiEPN #marchaAntiEPN #marchaAntiEPN." Such repetition, particularly by accounts already showing suspiciously bot-like behavior, triggers systems within Twitter that identify attempts to manipulate the hashtagging system and then remove the hashtags in question from the Trending Topics list. In other words, because the items in Trending Topics become newsworthy and attract attention, spammers and advertisers will try to push hashtags up into that space through repetition, so Twitter has developed mechanisms for spotting and blocking such activity.[12]

The Mexican-election Twitter bots were deliberately engaging in bad behavior in order to trigger an automatic delisting, thereby keeping the impact of #marchaAntiEPN "off the radar" of the larger media. They were making the hashtag unusable and removing its potential media significance. This was obfuscation as a destructive act. Though such efforts use the same basic tactic as radar chaff (that is, producing many imitations configured to hide the real thing), they have very different goals: rather than just buying time (for example, in the run-up to an election and during the period of unrest afterward), they render certain terms unusable—even, from the perspective of a sorting algorithm, toxic—by manipulating the properties of the data through the use of false signals.

1.3 CacheCloak: location services without location tracking

CacheCloak takes an approach to obfuscation that is suited to location-based services (LBSs).[13] It illustrates two twists in the use of false echoes and imitations in obfuscation. The first of these is making sure that relevant data can still be extracted by the user; the second is trying to find an approach that can work indefinitely rather than as a temporary time-buying strategy.

Location-based services take advantage of the locative capabilities of mobile devices to create various services, some of them social (e.g., Four-Square, which turns going places into a competitive game), some lucrative (e.g., location-aware advertising), and some thoroughly useful (e.g., maps and nearest-object searches). The classic rhetoric of balancing privacy against utility, in which utility is often presented as detrimental to privacy, is evident here. If you want the value of an LBS—for example, if you want to be on the network that your friends are on so you can meet with one of them if you and that person are near one another—you will have to sacrifice some privacy, and you will have to get accustomed to having the service provider know where you are. CacheCloak suggests a way to reconfigure the tradeoff.

"Where other methods try to obscure the user's path by hiding parts of it," the creators of CacheCloak write, "we obscure the user's location by surrounding it with other users' paths"[14]—that is, through the propagation of ambiguous data. In the standard model, your phone sends your location to the service and gets the information you requested in return. In the CacheCloak model, your phone predicts your possible paths and then fetches the results for several likely routes. As you move, you receive the benefits of locative awareness—access to what you are looking for, in the form of data cached in advance of potential requests—and an adversary is left with many possible paths, unable to distinguish the beginning from the end of a route and unable to determine where you came from, where you mean to go, or even where you are. From an observer's perspective, the salient data—the data we wish to keep to ourselves—are buried inside a space of other, equally likely data.

1.4 TrackMeNot: blending genuine and artificial search queries

TrackMeNot, developed in 2006 by Daniel Howe, Helen Nissenbaum, and Vincent Toubiana, exemplifies a software strategy for concealing activity with imitative signals.[15] The purpose of TrackMeNot is to foil the profiling of users through their searches. It was designed in response to the U.S. Department of Justice's request for Google's search logs and in response to the surprising discovery by a *New York Times* reporter that some identities and profiles could be inferred even from anonymized search logs published by AOL Inc.[16]

Our search queries end up acting as lists of locations, names, interests, and problems. Whether or not our full IP addresses are included, our identities can be inferred from these lists, and patterns in our interests can be discerned. Responding to calls for accountability, search companies have offered ways to address people's concerns about the collection and storage of search queries, though they continue to collect and analyze logs of such queries.[17] Preventing any stream of queries from being inappropriately revealing of a particular person's interests and activities remains a challenge.[18]

The solution TrackMeNot offers is not to hide users' queries from search engines (an impractical method, in view of the need for query satisfaction), but to obfuscate by automatically generating queries from a "seed list" of terms. Initially culled from RSS feeds, these terms evolve so that different users develop different seed lists. The precision of the imitation is continually refined by repopulating the seed list with new terms generated from returns to search queries. TrackMeNot submits queries in a manner that tries to mimic real users' search behaviors. For example, a user who has searched for "good wi-fi cafe chelsea" may also have searched for "savannah kennels," "freshly pressed juice miami," "asian property firm," "exercise delays dementia," and "telescoping halogen light." The activities of individuals are masked by those of many ghosts, making the pattern harder to discern so that it becomes much more difficult to say of any query that it was a product of human intention rather than an automatic output of TrackMeNot. In this way, TrackMeNot extends the role of obfuscation, in some situations, to include plausible deniability.

1.5 Uploads to leak sites: burying significant files

WikiLeaks used a variety of systems for securing the identities of both visitors and contributors. However, there was a telltale sign that could undercut the safety of the site: uploads of files. If snoops could monitor the traffic on WikiLeaks, they could identify acts of submitting material to WikiLeaks' secure server. Especially if they could make informed guesses as to the compressed sizes of various collections of subsequently released data, they could retroactively draw inferences as to what was transmitted, when it was transmitted, and (in view of failures in other areas of technical and operations security) by whom it was transmitted. Faced with this very particular kind of challenge, WikiLeaks developed a script to produce false signals. It launched in the browsers of visitors, generating activity that looked like uploads to the secure server.[19] A snoop would therefore see an enormous mob of apparent leakers (the vast majority of whom were, in actuality, merely reading or looking through documents already made available), a few of whom might really be leakers. It didn't seek to provide *particular* data to interfere with data mining or with advertising; it simply sought to imitate and conceal the movements of some of its users.

Even encrypted and compressed data contain pertinent metadata, however, and the proposal for OpenLeaks—an ultimately unsuccessful variant on WikiLeaks, developed by some of the disaffected participants in the original WikiLeaks system—includes a further refinement.[20] After a statistical analysis of the WikiLeaks submissions, OpenLeaks developed a model of fake uploads that would keep to the same ratios of *sizes* of files typically appearing in the upload traffic of a leak site. Most of the files ranged in size from 1.5 to 2 megabytes, though a few outliers exceeded 700 megabytes. If an adversary can monitor upload traffic, form can be as telling as content, and as useful in sorting real signals from fake ones. As this example suggests, obfuscation mechanisms can gain a great deal from figuring out all the parameters that can be manipulated—and from figuring out what the adversary is looking for, so as to give the adversary a manufactured version of it.

1.6 False tells: making patterns to trick a trained observer

Consider how the same basic pattern of obfuscation can be called to service in a context lighter than concealing the work of whistleblowers: poker.

Much of the pleasure and much of the challenge of poker lies in learning to infer from expressions, gestures, and body language whether someone is bluffing (that is, pretending to hold a hand weaker than the one he or she actually holds) in hopes of drawing a call. Central to the work of studying one's opponents is the "tell"—some unconscious habit or tic that an opponent displays in response to a strong or a weak hand, such as sweating, glancing worriedly, or leaning forward. Tells are so important in the informational economy of poker that players sometimes use *false tells*—that is, they create mannerisms that may appear to be parts of a larger pattern.[21] In common poker strategy, the use of a false tell is best reserved for a crucial moment in a tournament, lest the other players figure out that it is inaccurate and use it against you in turn. A patient analysis of multiple games could separate the true tells from the false ones, but in the time-bound context of a high-stakes game the moment of falsehood can be highly effective. Similar techniques are used in many sports that involve visible communication. One example is signaling in baseball—as a coach explained to a newspaper reporter, "Sometimes you're giving a sign, but it doesn't even mean anything."[22]

1.7 Group identity: many people under one name

One of the simplest and most memorable examples of obfuscation, and one that introduces the work of the *group* in obfuscation, is the scene in the film *Spartacus* in which the rebel slaves are asked by Roman soldiers to identify their leader, whom the soldiers intend to crucify.[23] As Spartacus (played by Kirk Douglas) is about to speak, one by one the others around him say "I am Spartacus!" until the entire crowd is claiming that identity.

Many people assuming the same identity for group protection (for example, Captain Swing in the English agricultural uprisings of 1830, the ubiquitous "Jacques" adopted by the radicals in Dickens's *A Tale of Two Cities*, or the Guy Fawkes mask in the graphic novel *V for Vendetta*, now associated with the hacktivist group known as Anonymous) is, at this point, almost a cliché.[24] Marco Deseriis has studied the use of "improper names" and collective identities in the effacement of individual responsibility and the proliferation of action.[25] Some forms of obfuscation can be conducted solo; others rely on groups, teams, communities, and confederates.

1.8 Identical confederates and objects: many people in one outfit

There are many examples of obfuscation by members of a group working in concert to produce genuine but misleading signals within which the genuine, salient signal is concealed. One memorable example from popular culture is the scene in the 1999 remake of the film *The Thomas Crown Affair* in which the protagonist, wearing a distinctive Magritte-inspired outfit, is suddenly in a carefully orchestrated mass of other men, dressed in the same outfit, circulating through the museum and exchanging their identical briefcases.[26] The bank-robbery scheme in the 2006 film *Inside Man* hinges on the robbers' all wearing painters' overalls, gloves, and masks and dressing their hostages the same way.[27] Finally, consider the quick thinking of Roger Thornhill, the protagonist of Alfred Hitchcock's 1959 film *North By Northwest*, who, in order to evade the police when his train arrives in Chicago, bribes a redcap (a baggage handler) to lend him his distinctive uniform, knowing that the crowd of redcaps at the station will give the police too much of something specific to look for.[28]

Identical objects as modes of obfuscation are common enough and sufficiently understood to recur in imagination and in fact. The *ancilia* of ancient Rome exemplify this. A shield (*ancile*) fell from the sky—so the legend goes—during the reign of Numa Pompilius, Rome's second king (753–673 BCE), and was interpreted as a sign of divine favor, a sacred relic whose ownership would guarantee Rome's continued imperium.[29] It was hung in the Temple of Mars along with eleven exact duplicates, so would-be thieves wouldn't know which one to take. The six plaster busts of Napoleon from which the Sherlock Holmes story gets its title offers another example. The villain sticks a black pearl into the wet plaster of an object that not only has five duplicates but also is one of a larger class of objects (cheap white busts of Napoleon) that are ubiquitous enough to be invisible.[30]

A real-world instance is provided by the so-called Craigslist robber. At 11 a.m. on Tuesday, September 30, 2008, a man dressed as an exterminator (in a blue shirt, goggles, and a dust mask), and carrying a spray pump, approached an armored car parked outside a bank in Monroe, Washington, incapacitated the guard with pepper spray, and made off with the money.[31] When the police arrived, they found thirteen men in the area wearing blue shirts, goggles, and dust masks—a uniform they were wearing on the instructions of a Craigslist ad that promised a good wage for maintenance work, which was to start at 11:15 a.m. at the bank's address. It would have taken only a few minutes to determine that none of the day laborers was the robber, but a few minutes was all the time the robber needed.

Then there is the powerful story, often retold though factually inaccurate, of the king of Denmark and a great number of Danish gentiles wearing the Yellow Star so that the occupying Germans couldn't distinguish and deport Danish Jews. Although the Danes courageously protected their Jewish population in other ways, the Yellow Star wasn't used by the Nazis in occupied Denmark, for fear of arousing more anti-German feeling. However, "there were documented cases of non–Jews wearing yellow stars to protest Nazi anti–Semitism in Belgium, France, the Netherlands, Poland, and even Germany itself."[32] This legend offers a perfect example of cooperative obfuscation: gentiles wearing the Yellow Star as an act of protest, providing a population into which individual Jews could blend.[33]

1.9 Excessive documentation: making analysis inefficient

Continuing our look at obfuscation that operates by adding in genuine but misleading signals, let us now consider the overproduction of documents as a form of obfuscation, as in the case of over-disclosure of material in a lawsuit. This was the strategy of Augustin Lejeune, chief of the General Police Bureau in the Committee of Public Safety, a major instrument in the Terror phase of the French Revolution. Lejeune and his clerks produced the reports that laid the groundwork for arrests, internments, and executions. Later, in an effort to excuse his role in the Terror, Lejeune argued that the exacting, overwhelmingly detailed quality of the reports from his office had been deliberate: he had instructed his clerks to overproduce material, and to report "the most minor details," in order to slow the production of intelligence for the Committee without the appearance of rebellion. It is doubtful that Lejeune's claims are entirely accurate (the numbers he cites for the production of reports aren't reliable), but, as Ben Kafka points out, he had come up with a bureaucratic strategy for creating slowdowns through oversupply: "He seems to have recognized, if only belatedly, that the proliferation of documents and details presented opportunities for resistance, as well as for compliance."[34] In situations where one can't say No, there are opportunities for a chorus of unhelpful Yeses—for example, don't send a folder in response to a request; send a pallet of boxes of folders containing potentially relevant papers.

1.10 Shuffling SIM cards: rendering mobile targeting uncertain

As recent reporting and some of Edward Snowden's disclosures have revealed, analysts working for the National Security Agency use a combination of signals-intelligence sources—particularly cell-phone metadata and data from geolocation systems—to identify and track targets for elimination.[35] The metadata (showing what numbers were called and when they were called) produce a model of a social network that makes it possible to identify particular phone numbers as belonging to persons of interest; the geolocative properties of mobile phones mean that these numbers can be situated, with varying degrees of accuracy, in particular places, which can then be targeted by drones. In other words, this system can proceed from identification to location to assassination without ever having a face-to-face visual identification of a person. The closest a drone operator may come to setting eyes on someone may be the exterior of a building, or a silhouette getting into a car. In view of the spotty records of the NSA's cell-phone-metadata program and the drone strikes, there are, of course, grave concerns about accuracy. Whether one is concerned about threats to national security remaining safe and active, about the lives of innocent people taken unjustly, or about both, it is easy to see the potential flaws in this approach.

Let us flip the situation, however, and consider it more abstractly from the perspective of the targets. Most of the NSA's targets are obligated to always have, either with or near them, a tracking device (only the very highest-level figures in terrorist organizations are able to be free of signals-generating technology), as are virtually all the people with whom they are in contact. The calls and conversations that sustain their organizations also provide the means of their identification; the structure that makes their work possible also traps them. Rather than trying to coordinate anti-aircraft guns to find a target somewhere in the sky, the adversary has complete air superiority, able to deliver a missile to a car, a street corner, or a house. However, the adversary also has a closely related set of systemic limitations. This system, remarkable as it is in scope and capabilities, ultimately relies on SIM (subscriber identity module) cards and on physical possession of mobile phones—a kind of narrow bandwidth that can be exploited. A former drone operator for the Joint Special Operations Command has reported that targets therefore take measures to mix and confuse genuine signals. Some individuals have many SIM cards associated with their identity in circulation, and the cards are randomly redistributed. One approach is to hold meetings at which all the attendees put their SIM cards into a bag, then pull cards from the bag at random, so that who is actually connected to each device will not be clear. (This is a time-bound approach: if metadata analysis is sufficiently sophisticated, an analyst should eventually be able to sort the individuals again on the basis of past calling patterns, but irregular re-shuffling renders that more difficult.) Re-shuffling may also happen unintentionally as targets who aren't aware that they are being tracked sell their phones or lend them to friends or relatives. The end result is a system with enormous technical precision and a very uncertain rate of actual success, whether measured in terms of dangerous individuals eliminated or in terms of innocent noncombatants killed by mistake. Even when fairly exact location tracking and social-graph analysis can't be avoided, using obfuscation to mingle and mix genuine signals, rather than generating false signals, can offer a measure of defense and control.

1.11 Tor relays: requests on behalf of others that conceal personal traffic

Tor is a system designed to facilitate anonymous use of the Internet through a combination of encryption and passing the message through many different independent "nodes." In a hybrid strategy of obfuscation, Tor can be used in combination with other, more powerful mechanisms for concealing data. Such a strategy achieves obfuscation partially through the mixing and interleaving of genuine (encrypted) activity. Imagine a message passed surreptitiously through a huge crowd to you. The message is a question without any identifying information; as far as you know, it was written by the last person to hold it, the person who handed it to you. The reply you write and pass back vanishes into the crowd, following an unpredictable path. Somewhere in that crowd, the writer receives his answer. Neither you nor anyone else knows exactly who the writer was.

If you request a Web page while working through Tor, your request will not come from your IP address; it will come from an "exit node" (analogous to the last person who hands the message to its addressee) on the Tor system, along with the requests of many other Tor users. Data enter the Tor system and pass into a labyrinth of relays—that is, computers on the Tor network (analogous to people in the crowd) that offer some of their bandwidth for the purpose of handling Tor traffic from others, agreeing to pass messages sight unseen. The more relays there are, the faster the system is as a whole. If you are already using Tor to protect your Internet traffic, you can turn your computer into a relay for the collective greater good. Both the Tor network and the obfuscation of individuals on the network improve as more people make use of the network.

Obfuscation, Tor's designers point out, augments its considerable protective power. In return for running a Tor relay, "you do get better anonymity against some attacks. The simplest example is an attacker who owns a small number of Tor relays. He will see a connection from you, but he won't be able to know whether the connection originated at your computer or was relayed from somebody else."[36] If someone has agents in the crowd—that is, if someone is running Tor relays for surveillance purposes—the agents can't read a message they pass, but they can notice who passed it to them. If you are on Tor and not running a relay, they know that you wrote the message you gave to them. But if you are letting your computer operate as a relay, the message may be yours or may be just one among many that you are passing on for other people. Did that message start with you, or not? The information is now ambiguous, and messages you have written are safe in a flock of other messages you pass along. This is, in short, a significantly more sophisticated and efficient way to render particular data transactions ambiguous and to thwart traffic analysis by making use of the volume of the traffic. It doesn't merely mix genuine signals (as shaking up SIM cards in a bag does, with all the consequent problems of coordination); it gets each message to its destination. However, each message can serve to make the sources of other messages uncertain.

1.12 Babble tapes: hiding speech in speech

An old cliché about mobsters under threat from the FBI involved a lot of talking in bathrooms: the splash and hiss of water and the hum of the ventilation fan, so the story went, made conversations hard to hear if the house was bugged or if someone in the room was wearing a wire. There are now refined (and much more effective) techniques for defeating audio surveillance that draw more directly on obfuscation. One of these is the use of so-called babble tapes.[37] Paradoxically, babble tapes have been used less by mobsters than by attorneys concerned that eavesdropping may violate attorney-client privilege.

A babble tape is a digital file meant to be played in the background during conversations. The file is complex. Forty voice tracks run simultaneously (thirty-two in English, eight in other languages), and each track is compressed in frequency and time to produce additional "voices" that fill the entire frequency spectrum. There are also various non-human mechanical noises, and a periodic supersonic burst (inaudible to adult listeners) engineered specifically to interfere with the automatic gain-control system of an eavesdropping device configures itself to best pick up an audio signal. Most pertinent for present purposes, the voices on a babble tape used by an attorney include those of the client and the attorney themselves. The dense mélange of voices increases the difficulty of discerning any single voice.

1.13 Operation Vula: obfuscation in the struggle against Apartheid

We close this chapter with a detailed narrative example of obfuscation employed in a complex context by a group seeking to get Nelson Mandela released from prison in South Africa during the struggle against Apartheid. Called Operation Vula (short for Vul'indlela, meaning Opening the Road), it was devised by leaders of the African National Congress within South Africa who were in contact with Mandela and were coordinating their efforts with those of ANC agents, sympathizers, and generals around the world.

The last project of this scale that the ANC had conducted had resulted in the catastrophe of the early 1960s in which Mandela and virtually all of the ANC's top leaders had been arrested and the Liliesleaf Farm documents had been captured and had been used against them in court. This meant that Operation Vula had to be run with absolutely airtight security and privacy practices. Indeed, when the full scope of the operation was revealed in the 1990s, it came as a surprise not just to the South African government and to international intelligence services but also to many prominent leadership figures within the ANC. People purportedly receiving kidney transplants or recovering from motorcycle accidents had actually gone deep underground with new identities and then had returned to South Africa, "opening the road" for Mandela's release. Given the surveillance inside and outside South Africa, the possible compromise of pre-existing ANC communications channels, and the interest of spies and law-enforcement groups around the world, Operation Vula had to have secure ways of sharing and coordinating information.

The extraordinary tale of Operation Vula has been told by one of its chief architects, Tim Jenkin, in the pages of the ANC's journal *Mayibuye*.[38] It represents a superb example of operations security, tradecraft, and managing a secure network.

Understanding when and how obfuscation came to be employed in Operation Vula requires understanding some of the challenges its architects faced. Using fixed phone lines within South Africa, each linked to an address and a name, wasn't an option. The slightest compromise might lead to wiretaps and to what we would now call metadata analysis, and thus a picture of the activist network could be put together from domestic and overseas phone logs. The Vula agents had various coding systems, each of them hampered by the difficulty and tedium of doing the coding by hand. There was always the temptation to fall back on "speaking in whispers over phones again," especially when crises happened and things began moving fast. The operation had to be seamlessly coordinated between South Africa (primarily Durban and Johannesburg) and Lusaka, London, Amsterdam, and other locations around the world as agents circulated. Postal service was slow and vulnerable, encrypting was enormously time consuming and often prone to sloppiness, use of home phones was forbidden, and coordinating between multiple time zones around the world seemed impossible.

Jenkin was aware of the possibilities of using personal computers to make encryption faster and more efficient. Based in London after his escape from Pretoria Central Prison, he spent the mid 1980s working on the communications system needed for Operation Vula, which ultimately evolved into a remarkable network. Encryption happened on a personal computer, and the ciphered message was then expressed as a rapid series of tones recorded onto a portable cassette player. An agent would go to a public pay phone and dial a London number, which would be picked up by an answering machine that Jenkin had modified to record for up to five minutes. The agent would play the cassette into the mouthpiece of the phone. The tones, recorded on the cassette's other side, could be played through an acoustic modem into the computer and then decrypted. (There was also an "outgoing" answering machine. Remote agents could call from a pay phone, record the tones for their messages, and decrypt them anywhere they had access to a computer that could run the ciphering systems Jenkin had devised.)

This was already an enormously impressive network—not least because large parts of its digital side (including a way of implementing error-handling codes to deal with the noise of playing back messages over international phone lines from noisy booths) had to be invented from scratch. However, as Operation Vula continued to grow and the network of operatives to expand, the sheer quantity of traffic threatened to overwhelm the network. Operatives were preparing South Africa for action, and that work didn't leave a lot of time for finding pay phones that accepted credit cards (the sound of coins dropping could interfere with the signal) and standing around with tape players. Jenkin and his collaborators would stay up late, changing tapes in the machines as the messages poured in. The time had come to switch to encrypted email, but the whole system had been developed to avoid the use of known, owned telephone lines within South Africa.

Operation Vula needed to be able to send encrypted messages to and from computers in South Africa, in Lukasa, and in London without arousing suspicion. During the 1980s, while the network we have described was taking shape, the larger milieu of international business was producing exactly the kind of background against which this subterfuge could hide itself. The question was, as Jenkin put it, "Did the enemy have the capacity to determine which of the thousands of messages leaving the country every day was a 'suspicious' one?" The activists needed a typical user of encrypted email—one without clear political affiliation—to find out if their encrypted messages could escape notice in the overall tide of mail. They needed, Jenkin later recalled, to "find someone who would normally use a computer for communicating abroad and get that person to handle the communications."

They had an agent who could try this system out before they switched their communications over to the new approach: a native South African who was about to return to his homeland after working abroad for many years as a programmer for British telecommunications companies. Their agent would behave just as a typical citizen sending a lot of email messages every day would, using a commercial email provider rather than a custom server and relying on the fact that many businesses used encryption in their communications. "This was a most normal thing for a person in his position to do," Jenkin recalled. The system worked: the agent's messages blended in with the ordinary traffic, providing a platform for openly secret communications that could be expanded rapidly.

Posing as computer consultants, Tim Jenkin and Ronnie Press (another important member of the ANC Technical Committee) were able to keep abreast of new devices and storage technologies, and to arrange for their purchase and delivery where they were needed. Using a combination of commercial email providers and bulletin-board services run off personal and pocket computers, they were able to circulate messages within South Africa and around the world, and also to prepare fully formatted ANC literature for distribution. (The system even carried messages from Mandela, smuggled out by his lawyer in secret compartments in books and typed into the system.) The ordinary activity of ordinary users with bland business addresses became a high-value informational channel, moving huge volumes of encrypted data from London to Lukasa and then into South Africa and between Vula cells in that country. The success of this system was due in part to historical circumstance—personal computers and email (including encrypted email) had become common enough to avoid provoking suspicion, but not so common as to inspire the construction of new, more comprehensive digital surveillance systems such as governments have today.

The Vula network, in its ultimate stage, wasn't naive about the security of digital messages; it kept everything protected by a sophisticated encryption system full of inventive details, and it encouraged its users to change their encryption keys and to practice good operations security. Within that context, however, it offers an excellent example of the role obfuscation can play in building a secure and secret communications system. It illustrates the benefits of finding the right existing situation and blending into it, lost in the hubbub of ordinary commerce, hidden by the crowd.

2 OTHER EXAMPLES

2.1 Orb-weaving spiders: obfuscating animals

Some animals (and some plants too) have ways to conceal themselves or engage in visual trickery. Insects mimic the appearance of leaves or twigs, rabbits have countershading (white bellies) to eliminate the cues of shape that enables a hawk to easily see and strike, and spots on buttterflies' wings mimic the eyes of predatory animals.

A quintessential obfuscator in the animal world is *Cyclosa mulmeinensis*, an orb-weaving spider.[1] This spider faces a particular problem for which obfuscation is a sound solution: its web must be somewhat exposed in order to catch prey, but that makes the spider much more vulnerable to attack by wasps. The spider's solution is to make stand-ins for itself out of remains of its prey, leaf litter, and spider silk, with (from the perspective of a wasp) the same size, color, and reflectivity of the spider itself, and to position these decoys around the web. This decreases the odds of a wasp strike hitting home and gives *Cyclosa mulmeinensis* time to scuttle out of harm's way.

2.2 False orders: using obfuscation to attack rival businesses

The obfuscation goal of making a channel noisier can be employed not only to conceal significant traffic, but also to raise the costs of organization through that channel—and so raise the cost of doing business. The taxi-replacement company Uber provides an example of this approach in practice.

The market for businesses that provide something akin to taxis and car services is growing fast, and competition for both customers and drivers is fierce. Uber has offered bonuses to recruit drivers from competing services, and rewards merely for visiting the company's headquarters. In New York, Uber pursued a particularly aggressive strategy against its competitor Gett, using obfuscation to recruit Gett's drivers.[2] Over the course of a few days, several Uber employees would order rides from Gett, then would cancel those orders shortly before the Gett drivers arrived. This flood of fruitless orders kept the Gett drivers in motion, not earning fees, and unable to fulfill many legitimate requests. Shortly after receiving a fruitless order, or several of them, a Gett driver would receive a text message from Uber offering him money to switch jobs. Real requests for rides were effectively obfuscated by Uber's fake requests, which reduced the value of a job with Gett. (Lyft, a ridesharing company, has alleged that Uber has made similar obfuscation attacks on its drivers.)

2.3 French decoy radar emplacements: defeating radar detectors

Obfuscation plays a part in the French government's strategy against radar detectors.[3] These fairly common appliances warn drivers when police are using speed-detecting radar nearby. Some radar detectors can indicate the position of a radar gun relative to a user's vehicle, and thus are even more effective in helping drivers to avoid speeding tickets.

In theory, tickets are a disincentive to excessively fast and dangerous driving; in practice, they serve as a revenue source for local police departments and governments. For both reasons, police are highly motivated to defeat radar detectors.

The option of regulating or even banning radar detectors is unrealistic in view of the fact that 6 million French drivers are estimated to own them. Turning that many ordinary citizens into criminals seems impolitic. Without the power to stop surveillance of radar guns, the French government has taken to obfuscation to render such surveillance less useful in high-traffic zones by deploying arrays of devices that trigger radar detectors' warning signals without actually measuring speed. These devices mirror the chaff strategy in that the warning chirps multiply and multiply again. One of them may, indeed, indicate actual speed-detecting radar, but which one? The meaningful signal is drowned in a mass of other plausible signals. Either drivers risk getting speeding tickets or they slow down in response to the deluge of radar pings. And the civic goal is accomplished. No matter how one feels about traffic cops or speeding drivers, the case holds interest as a way obfuscation serves to promote an end not by destroying one's adversaries' devices outright but by rendering them functionally irrelevant.

2.4 AdNauseam: clicking all the ads

In a strategy resembling that of the French radar-gun decoys, AdNauseam, a browser plug-in, resists online surveillance for purposes of behavioral advertising by clicking all the banner ads on all the Web pages visited by its users. In conjunction with Ad Block Plus, AdNauseam functions in the background, quietly clicking all blocked ads while recording, for the user's interest, details about ads that have been served and blocked.

The idea for AdNauseam emerged out of a sense of helplessness: it isn't possible to stop ubiquitous tracking by ad networks, or to comprehend the intricate institutional and technical complexities constituting its socio-technical backend. These include Web cookies and beacons, browser fingerprinting (which uses combinations and configurations of the visitor's technology to identify their activities), ad networks, and analytics companies. Efforts to find some middle ground through a Do Not Track technical standard have been frustrated by powerful actors in the political economy of targeted advertising. In this climate of no compromise, AdNauseam was born. Its design was inspired by a slender insight into the prevailing business model, which charges prospective advertisers a premium for delivering viewers with proven interest in their products. What more telling evidence is there of interest than clicks on particular ads? Clicks also sometimes constitute the basis of payment to an ad network and to the ad-hosting website. Clicks on ads, in combination with other data streams, build up the profiles of tracked users. Like the French radar decoy systems, AdNauseam isn't aiming to destroy the ability to track clicks; instead it functions by diminishing the value of those clicks by obfuscating the real clicks with clicks that it generates automatically.

2.5 Quote stuffing: confusing algorithmic trading strategies

The term "quote stuffing" has been applied to bursts of anomalous activity on stock exchanges that appear to be misleading trading data generated to gain advantage over competitors on the exchange. In the rarefied field of high-frequency trading (HFT), algorithms perform large volumes of trades far faster than humans could, taking advantage of minute spans of time and differences in price that wouldn't draw the notice of attention of human traders. Timing has always been critical to trading, but in HFT thousandths of a second separate profit and loss, and complex strategies have emerged to accelerate your trades and retard those of your competitors. Analysts of market behavior began to notice unusual patterns of HFT activity during the summer of 2010: bursts of quote requests for a particular stock, sometimes thousands of them in a second. Such activity seemed to have no economic rationale, but one of the most interesting and plausible theories is that these bursts are an obfuscation tactic. One observer explains the phenomenon this way: "If you could generate a large number of quotes that your competitors have to process, but you can ignore since you generated them, you gain valuable processing time."[4]

Unimportant information, in the form of quotes, is used to crowd the field of salient activity so that the generators of the unimportant information can accurately assess what is happening while making it more difficult and time consuming for their competitors to do so. They create a cloud that only they can see through. None of the patterns in that information would fool or even distract an analyst over a longer period of time—it would be obvious that they were artificial and insignificant. But in the sub-split-second world of HFT, the time it takes merely to observe and process activity makes all the difference.

If the use of "quote stuffing" were to spread, it might threaten the very integrity of the stock market as a working system by overwhelming the physical infrastructure on which the stock exchanges rely with hundreds of thousands of useless quotes consuming bandwidth. "This is an extremely disturbing development," the observer quoted above adds, "because as more HFT systems start doing this, it is only a matter of time before quote-stuffing shuts down the entire market from congestion."[5]

2.6 Swapping loyalty cards to interfere with analysis of shopping patterns

Grocery stores have long been in the technological vanguard when it comes to working with data. Relatively innocuous early loyalty-card programs were used to draw repeat customers, extracting extra profit margins from people who didn't use the card and aiding primitive data projects such as organizing direct mailings by ZIP code. The vast majority of grocers and chains outsourced the business of analyzing data to ACNielsen, Catalina Marketing, and a few other companies.[6] Although these practices were initially perceived as isolated and inoffensive, a few incidents altered the perception of purpose from innocuous and helpful to somewhat sinister.

In 1999, a slip-and-fall accident in a Los Angeles supermarket led to a lawsuit, and attorneys for the supermarket chain threatened to disclose the victim's history of alcohol purchases to the court.[7] A string of similar cases over the years fed a growing suspicion in the popular imagination that so-called loyalty cards were serving ends beyond the allotment of discounts. Soon after their widespread introduction, card-swapping networks developed. People shared cards in order to obfuscate data about their purchasing patterns— initially in *ad hoc* physical meetings, then, with the help of mailing lists and online social networks, increasingly in large populations and over wide geographical regions. Rob's Giant Bonus Card Swap Meet, for instance, started from the idea that a system for sharing bar codes could enable customers of the DC-area supermarket chain Giant to print out the bar codes of other customers and then paste them onto their cards.[8] Similarly, the Ultimate Shopper project fabricated and distributed stickers imprinted with the bar code from a Safeway loyalty card, thereby creating "an army of clones" whose shopping data would be accrued.[9] Cardexchange.org, devoted to exchanging loyalty cards by mail, presents itself as a direct analogue to physical meet-ups held for the same purpose. The swapping of loyalty cards constitutes obfuscation as a group activity: the greater the number of people who are willing to share their cards, and the farther the cards travel, the less reliable the data become.

Card-swapping websites also host discussions and post news articles and essays about differing approaches to loyalty-card obfuscation and some of the ethical issues they raise. Negative effects on grocery stores are of concern, as card swapping degrades the data available to them and perhaps to other recipients. It is worth noting that such effects are contingent both on the card programs and on the approaches to card swapping. For example, sharing of a loyalty card within a household or among friends, though it may deprive a store of individual-level data, may still provide some useful information about shopping episodes or about product preferences within geographic areas. The value of data at the scale of a postal code, a neighborhood, or a district is far from insignificant. And there may be larger patterns to be inferred from the genuine information present in mixed and mingled data.

2.7 BitTorrent Hydra: using fake requests to deter collection of addresses

BitTorrent Hydra, a now-defunct but interesting and illustrative project, fought the surveillance efforts of anti-file-sharing interests by mixing genuine requests for bits of a file with dummy requests.[10] The BitTorrent protocol broke a file into many small pieces and allowed users to share files with one another by simultaneously sending and receiving the pieces.[11] Rather than download an entire file from another user, one assembled it from pieces obtained from anyone else who had them, and anyone who needed a piece that you had could get it from you. This many-pieces-from-many-people approach expedited the sharing of files of all kinds and quickly became the method of choice for moving large files, such as those containing movies and music.[12] To help users of BitTorrent assemble the files they needed, "torrent trackers" logged IP addresses that were sending and receiving files. For example, if you were looking for certain pieces of a file, torrent trackers would point you to the addresses of users who had the pieces you needed. Representatives of the content industry, looking for violations of their intellectual property, began to run their own trackers to gather the addresses of major unauthorized uploaders and downloaders in order to stop them or even prosecute them. Hydra counteracted this tracking by adding random IP addresses drawn from those previously used for BitTorrent to the collection of addresses found by the torrent tracker. If you had requested pieces of a file, you would be periodically directed to a user who didn't have what you were looking for. Although a small inefficiency for the BitTorrent system as a whole, it significantly undercut the utility of the addresses that copyright enforcers gathered, which may have belonged to actual participants but which may have been dummy addresses inserted by Hydra. Doubt and uncertainty had been reintroduced to the system, lessening the likelihood that one could sue with assurance. Rather than attempt to destroy the adversary's logs or to conceal BitTorrent traffic, Hydra provided an "I am Spartacus" defense. Hydra didn't avert data collection; however, by degrading the reliability of data collection, it called any specific findings into question.

2.8 Deliberately vague language: obfuscating agency

According to Jacquelyn Burkell and Alexandre Fortier, the privacy policies of health information sites use particularly obtuse linguistic constructions when describing their use of tracking, monitoring, and data collection.[13] Conditional verbs (e.g., "may"), passive voice, nominalization, temporal adverbs (e.g., "periodically" and "occasionally"), and the use of qualitative adjectives (as in "small piece of data") are among the linguistic constructions that Burkell and Fortier identify. As subtle as this form of obfuscation may seem, it is recognizably similar in operation to other forms we have already described: in place of a specific, specious denial (e.g., "we do not collect user information") or an exact admission, vague language produces many confusing gestures of possible activity and attribution. For example, the sentence "Certain information may be passively collected to connect use of this site with information about the use of other sites provided by third parties" puts the particulars of what a site does with certain information inside a cloud of possible interpretations.

These written practices veer away from obfuscation *per se* into the more general domain of abstruse language and "weasel words."[14] However, for purposes of illustrating the range of obfuscating approaches, the style of obfuscated language is useful: a document must be there, a straightforward denial isn't possible, and so the strategy becomes one of rendering who is doing what puzzling and unclear.

2.9 Obfuscation of anonymous text: stopping stylometric analysis

How much in text identifies it as the creation of one author rather than another? Stylometry uses only elements of linguistic style to attribute authorship to anonymous texts. It doesn't have to account for the possibility that only a certain person would have knowledge of some matter, for posts to an online forum, for other external clues (such as IP addresses), or for timing. It considers length of sentences, choice of words, and syntax, idiosyncrasies in formatting and usage, regionalisms, and recurrent typographical errors. It was a stylometric analysis that helped to settle the debate over the pseudonymous authors of the Federalist Papers (for example, the use of "while" versus "whilst" served to differentiate the styles of Alexander Hamilton and James Madison), and stylometry's usefulness in legal contexts is now well established.[15]

Given a small amount of text, stylometry can identify an author. And we mean small—according to Josyula Rao and Pankaj Ratangi, a sample consisting of about 6,500 words is sufficient (when used with a corpus of identified text, such as email messages, posts to a social network, or blog posts) to make possible an 80 percent rate of successful identification.[16] In the course of their everyday use of computers, many people produce 6,500 words in a few days.

Even if the goal is not to identify a specific author from a pool of known individuals, stylometry can produce information that is useful for purposes of surveillance. The technology activist Daniel Domscheit-Berg recalls the moment when he realized that if WikiLeaks' press releases, summaries of leaks, and other public texts were to undergo stylometric analysis it would show that only two people (Domscheit-Berg and Julian Assange) had been responsible for all those texts rather than a large and diverse group of volunteers, as Assange and Domscheit-Berg were trying to suggest.[17] Stylometric analysis offers an adversary a more accurate picture of an "anonymous" or secretive movement, and of its vulnerabilities, than can be gained by other means. Having narrowed authorship down to a small handful, the adversary is in a better position to target a known set of likely suspects.

Obfuscation makes it practicable to muddle the signal of a public body of text and to interfere with the process of connecting that body of text with a named author. Stylometric obfuscation is distinctive, too, in that its success is more readily tested than with many other forms of obfuscation, whose precise effects may be highly uncertain and/or may be known only to an uncooperative adversary.

Three approaches to beating stylometry offer useful insights into obfuscation. The first two, which are intuitive and straightforward, involve assuming a writing style that differs from one's usual style; their weaknesses highlight the value of using obfuscation.

Translation attacks take advantage of the weaknesses of machine translation by translating a text into multiple languages and then translating it back into its original language—a game of Telephone that might corrupt an author's style enough to prevent attribution.[18] Of course, this also renders the text less coherent and meaningful, and as translation tools improve it may not do a good enough job of depersonalization.

In *imitation attacks*, the original author deliberately writes a document in the style of another author. One vulnerability of that approach has been elegantly exposed by research.[19] Using the systems you would use to identify texts as belonging to the same author, you can determine the most powerful identifier of authorship between two texts, then eliminate that identifier from the analysis and look for the next-most-powerful identifier, then keep repeating the same process of elimination. If the texts really are by different people, accuracy in distinguishing between them will decline slowly, because beneath the big, obvious differences between one author and another there are many smaller and less reliable differences. If, however, both texts are by the same person, and one of them was written in imitation of another author, accuracy in distinguishing will decline rapidly, because beneath notable idiosyncrasies fundamental similarities are hard to shake.

Obfuscation attacks on stylometric analysis involve writing in such a way that there is no distinctive style. Researchers distinguish between "shallow" and "deep" obfuscation of texts. "Shallow" obfuscation changes only a small number of the most obvious features—for example, preference for "while" or for "whilst." "Deep" obfuscation runs the same system of classifiers used to defeat imitation, but does so for the author's benefit. Such a method might provide real-time feedback to an author editing a document, identifying the highest-ranked features and suggesting changes that would diminish the accuracy of stylometric analysis—for example, sophisticated paraphrasing. It might turn the banalities of "general usage" into a resource, enabling an author to blend into a vast crowd of similar authors.

Anonymouth—a tool that is under development as of this writing—is a step toward implementing this approach by producing statistically bland prose that can be obfuscated within the corpus of similar writing.[20] Think of the car provided to the getaway driver in the 2011 movie *Drive*: a silver late-model Chevrolet Impala, the most popular car in California, about which the mechanic promises "No one will be looking at you."[21] Ingenious as this may be, we wonder about a future in which political manifestos and critical documents strive for great rhetorical and stylistic banality and we lose the next Thomas Paine's equivalent to "These are the times that try men's souls."

2.10 Code obfuscation: baffling humans but not machines

In the field of computer programming, the term "obfuscated code" has two related but distinct meanings. The first is "obfuscation as a means of protection"—that is, making the code harder for human readers (or the various forms of "disassembly algorithms," which help explicate code that has been compiled for use) to interpret for purposes of copying, modification, or compromise. (A classic example of such reverse engineering goes as follows: Microsoft sends out a patch to update Windows computers for security purposes; bad actors get the patch and look at the code to figure out what vulnerability the patch is meant to address; they then devise an attack exploiting the vulnerability they have noticed hitting.) The second meaning of "obfuscated code" refers to a form of art: writing code that is fiendishly complex for a human to untangle but which ultimately performs a mundane computational task that is easily processed by a computer.

Simply put, a program that has been obfuscated will have the same functionality it had before, but will be more difficult for a human to analyze. Such a program exhibits two characteristics of obfuscation as a category and a concept. First, it operates under constraint—you obfuscate because people *will* be able to see your code, and the goals of obfuscation-as-protection are to decrease the efficiency of the analysis ("at least doubling the time needed," as experimental research has found), to reduce the gap between novices and skilled analysts, and to give systems that (for whatever reason) are easier to attack threat profiles closer to those of systems that are more difficult to attack.[22] Second, an obfuscated program's code uses strategies that are familiar from other forms of obfuscation: adding significant-seeming gibberish; having extra variables that must be accounted for; using arbitrary or deliberately confusing names for things within the code; including within the code deliberately confusing directions (essentially, "go to line x and do y") that lead to dead ends or wild goose chases; and various forms of scrambling. In its protective mode, code obfuscation is a time-buying approach to thwarting analysis—a speed bump. (Recently there have been advances that significantly increase the difficulty of de-obfuscation and the amount of time it requires; we will discuss them below.)

In its artistic, aesthetic form, code obfuscation is in the vanguard of counterintuitive, puzzling methods of accomplishing goals. Nick Montfort has described these practices in considerable detail.[23] For example, because of how the programming language C interprets names of variables, a programmer can muddle human analysis but not machine execution by writing code that includes the letters o and 0 in contexts that trick the eye by resembling zeroes. Some of these forms of obfuscation lie a little outside our working definition of "obfuscation," but they are useful for illustrating an approach to the fundamental problem of obfuscation: how to transform something that is open to scrutiny into something ambiguous, full of false leads, mistaken identities, and unmet expectations.

Code obfuscation, like stylometry, can be analyzed, tested, and optimized with precision. Its functionality is expanding from the limited scope of buying time and making the task of unraveling code more difficult to something closer to achieving complete opacity. A recent publication by Sanjam Garg and colleagues has moved code obfuscation from a "speed bump" to an "iron wall." A Multilinear Jigsaw Puzzle can break code apart so that it "fits together" like pieces of a puzzle. Although many arrangements are possible, only one arrangement is correct and represents the actual operation of the code.[24] A programmer can create a clean, clear, human-readable program and then run it through an obfuscator to produce something incomprehensible that can withstand scrutiny for a much longer time than before.

Code obfuscation—a lively, rich area for the exploration of obfuscation in general—seems to be progressing toward systems that are relatively easy to use and enormously difficult to defeat. This is even applicable to hardware: Jeyavijayan Rajendran and colleagues are utilizing components within circuits to create "logic obfuscation" in order to prevent reverse engineering of the functionality of a chip.[25]

2.11 Personal disinformation: strategies for individual disappearance

Disappearance specialists have much to teach would-be obfuscators. Many of these specialists are private detectives or "skip tracers"—professionals in the business of finding fugitives and debtors—who reverse engineer their own process to help their clients stay lost. Obviously many of the techniques and methods they employ have nothing to do with obfuscation, but rather are merely evasive or concealing—for instance, creating a corporation that can lease your new apartment and pay your bills so that your name will not be connected with those common and publicly searchable activities. However, in response to the proliferation of social networking and online presence, disappearance specialists advocate a strategy of *disinformation*, a variety of obfuscation. "Bogus individuals," to quote the disappearance consultant Frank Ahearn, can be produced in number and detail that will "bury" pre-existing personal information that might crop up in a list of Web search results.[26] This entails creating a few dozen fictitious people with the same name and the same basic characteristics, some of them with personal websites, some with accounts on social networks, and all of them intermittently active. For clients fleeing stalkers or abusive spouses, Ahearn recommends simultaneous producing numerous false leads that an investigator would be likely to follow—for example, a credit check for a lease on an apartment in one city (a lease that was never actually signed) and applications for utilities, employment addresses and phone numbers scattered across the country or the world, and a checking account, holding a fixed sum, with a debit card given to someone traveling to pay for expenses incurred in remote locations. Strategies suggested by disappearance specialists are based on known details about the adversary: the goal is not to make someone "vanish completely," but to put one far enough out of sight for practical purposes and thus to use up the seeker's budget and resources.

2.12 Apple's "cloning service" patent: polluting electronic profiling

In 2012, as part of a larger portfolio purchase from Novell, Apple acquired U.S. Patent 8,205,265, "Techniques to Pollute Electronic Profiling."[27] An approach to managing data surveillance without sacrificing services, it parallels several systems of technological obfuscation we have described already. This "cloning service" would automate and augment the process of producing misleading personal information, targeting online data collectors rather than private investigators.

A "cloning service" observes an individual's activities and assembles a plausible picture of his or her rhythms and interests. At the user's request, it will spin off a cloned identity that can use the identifiers provided to authenticate (to social networks, if not to more demanding observers) that represents a real person. These identifiers might include small amounts of actual confidential data (a few details of a life, such as hair color or marital status) mixed in with a considerable amount of deliberately inaccurate information. Starting from its initial data set, the cloned identity acquires an email address from which it will send and receive messages, a phone number (there are many online calling services that make phone numbers available for a small fee), and voicemail service. It may have an independent source of funds (perhaps a gift card or a debit card connected with a fixed account that gets refilled from time to time) that enables it to make small transactions. It may even have a mailing address or an Amazon locker—two more signals that suggest personhood. To these signals may be added some interests formally specified by the user and fleshed out with existing data made accessible by the scraping of social-network sites and by similar means. If a user setting up a clone were to select from drop-down menus that the clone is American and is interested in photography and camping, the system would figure out that the clone should be interested in the work of Ansel Adams. It can conduct searches (in the manner of TrackMeNot), follow links, browse pages, and even make purchases and establish accounts with services (e.g., subscribing to a mailing list devoted to deals on wilderness excursions, or following *National Geographic*'s Twitter account). These interests may draw on the user's actual interests, as inferred from things such as the user's browsing history, but may begin to diverge from those interests in a gradual, incremental way. (One could also salt the profile of one's clone with demographically appropriate activities, automatically chosen, building on the basics of one's actual data by selecting interests and behaviors so typical that they even out the telling idiosyncrasies of selfhood.)

After performing some straightforward analysis, a clone can also take on a person's rhythms and habits. If you are someone who is generally offline on weekends, evenings, and holidays, your clone will do likewise. It won't run continuously, and you can call it off if you are about to catch a flight, so an adversary will not be able to infer easily which activities are not yours. The clones will resume when you do. (For an explanation of why we now are talking about *multiple* clones, see below.) Of course, you can also select classes of activities in which your clones will not engage, lest the actors feigning to be you pirate some media content, begin to search for instructions on how to manufacture bombs, or look at pornography, unless they must do so to maintain plausibility—making all one's clones clean-living, serious-minded network users interested only in history, charitable giving, and recipes might raise suspicions. (The reason we have switched from talking about a singular clone to speaking about multiple clones is that once one clone is up and running there will be many others. Indeed, imagine a Borgesian joke in which sufficiently sophisticated clones, having learned from your history, demography, and habits, create clones of their own—copies of copies.) It is in your interest to expand this population of possible selves, leading lives that could be yours, day after day. This fulfills the fundamental goal outlined by the patent: your clones don't dodge or refuse data gathering, but in complying they pollute the data collected and reduce the value of profiles created from those data.

2.13 Vortex: cookie obfuscation as game and marketplace

Vortex—a proof-of-concept game (of sorts) developed by Rachel Law, an artist, designer, and programmer[28]—serves two functions simultaneously: to educate players about how online filtering systems affect their experience of the Internet and to confuse and misdirect targeted advertising based on browser cookies and other identifying systems. It functions as a game, serving to occupy and delight—an excellent venue for engaging users with a subject as seemingly dry and abstract as cookie-based targeted advertising. It is, in other words, a massively multi-player game of managing and exchanging personal data. The primary activities are "mining" cookies from websites and swapping them with other players. In one state of play, the game looks like a few color-coded buttons in the bookmarks bar of your browser that allow you to accumulate and swap between cookies (effectively taking on different identities); in another state of play, it looks like a landscape that represents a site as a quasi-planet that can be mined for cookies. (The landscape representation is loosely inspired by the popular exploration and building game Minecraft.)

Vortex ingeniously provides an entertaining and friendly way to display, manage, and share cookies. As you generate cookies, collect cookies, and swap cookies with other players, you can switch from one cookie to another with a click, thereby effectively disguising yourself and experiencing a different Web, a different set of filters, a different online self. This makes targeted advertising into a kind of choice: you can toggle over to cookies that present you as having a different gender, a different ethnicity, a different profession, and a different set of interests, and you can turn the ads and "personalized" details into mere background noise rather than distracting and manipulative components that peg you as some marketer's model of your identity. You can experience the Web as many different people, and you can make any record of yourself into a deniable portrait that doesn't have much to do with you in particular. In a trusted circle of friends, you can share account cookies that will enable you to purchase things that are embargoed in your location—for example, video streams that are available only to viewers in a certain country.

Hopping from self to self, and thereby ruining the process of compiling demographic dossiers, Vortex players would turn online identity into a field of options akin to the inventory screens of an online role-playing game. Instead of hiding, or giving up on the benefits that cookies and personalization can provide, Vortex allows users to deploy a crowd of identities while one's own identity is offered to a mob of others.

2.14 "Bayesian flooding" and "unselling" the value of online identity

In 2012, Kevin Ludlow, a developer and an entrepreneur, addressed a familiar obfuscation problem: What is the best way to hide data from Facebook?[29] The short answer is that there is no good way to *remove* data, and wholesale withdrawal from social networks isn't a realistic possibility for many users. Ludlow's answer is by now a familiar one.

"Rather than trying to hide information from Facebook," Ludlow wrote, "it may be possible simply to overwhelm it with too much information." Ludlow's experiment (which he called "Bayesian flooding," after a form of statistical analysis) entailed entering hundreds of life events into his Facebook Timeline over the course of months—events that added up to a life worthy of a three-volume novel. He got married and divorced, fought cancer (twice), broke numerous bones, fathered children, lived all over the world, explored a dozen religions, and fought for a slew of foreign militaries. Ludlow didn't expect anyone to fall for these stories; rather, he aimed to produce a less targeted personal experience of Facebook through the inaccurate guesses to which the advertising now responds, and as an act of protest against the manipulation and "coercive psychological tricks" embedded both in the advertising itself and in the site mechanisms that provoke or sway users to enter more information than they may intend to enter. In fact, the sheer implausibility of Ludlow's Timeline life as a globe-trotting, caddish mystic-mercenary with incredibly bad luck acts as a kind of filter: no human reader, and certainly no friend or acquaintance of Ludlow's, would assume that all of it was true, but the analysis that drives the advertising has no way of making such distinctions.

Ludlow hypothesizes that, if his approach were to be adopted more widely, it wouldn't be difficult to identify wild geographic, professional, or demographic outliers—people whose Timelines were much too crowded with incidents—and then wash their results out of a larger analysis. The particular understanding of victory that Ludlow envisions, which we discuss in the typology of goals presented in second part of this book, is a limited one. His Bayesian flooding isn't meant to counteract and corrupt the vast scope of data collection and analysis; rather, its purpose is to keep data about oneself both within the system and inaccessible. Max Cho describes a less extreme version: "The trick is to populate your Facebook with just enough lies as to destroy the value and compromise Facebook's ability to sell you"[30]—that is, to make your online activity harder to commoditize, as an act of conviction and protest.

2.15 FaceCloak: concealing the work of concealment

FaceCloak offers a different approach to limiting Facebook's access to personal information. When you create a Facebook profile and fill in your personal information, including where you live, where you went to school, your likes and dislikes, and so on, FaceCloak allows you to choose whether to display this information openly or to keep it private.[31] If you choose to display the information openly, it is passed to Facebook's servers. If you choose to keep it private, FaceCloak sends it to encrypted storage on a separate server, where it may be decrypted for and displayed only to friends you have authorized when they browse your Facebook page using the FaceCloak plug-in. Facebook never gains access to it.

What is salient about FaceCloak for present purposes is that it obfuscates its method by generating fake information for Facebook's required profile fields, concealing from Facebook and from unauthorized viewers the fact that the real data are stored elsewhere. As FaceCloak passes your real data to the private server, FaceCloak fabricates for Facebook a plausible non-person of a certain gender, with a name and an age, bearing no relation to the real facts about you. Under the cover of the plausible non-person, you can forge genuine connections with your friends while presenting obfuscated data for others.

2.16 Obfuscated likefarming: concealing indications of manipulation

Likefarming is now a well-understood strategy for generating the illusion of popularity on Facebook: employees, generally in the developing world, will "like" a particular brand or product for a fee (the going rate is a few U.S. dollars for a thousand likes).[32] A number of benefits accrue to heavily liked items— among other things, Facebook's algorithms will circulate pages that show evidence of popularity, thereby giving them additional momentum.

Likefarming is easy to spot, particularly for systems as sophisticated as Facebook's. It is performed in narrowly focused bursts of activity devoted to liking one thing or one family of things, from accounts that do little else. To appear more natural, they employ an obfuscating strategy of liking a spread of pages—generally pages recently added to the feed of Page Suggestions, which Facebook promotes according to its model of the user's interests.[33] The paid work of systematically liking one page can be hidden within scattered likes, appearing to come from a person with oddly singular yet characterless interests. Likefarming reveals the diversity of motives for obfuscation—not, in this instance, resistance to political domination, but simply provision of a service for a fee.

2.17 URME surveillance: "identity prosthetics" expressing protest

The artist Leo Selvaggio wanted to engage with the video surveillance of public space and the implications of facial-recognition software.[34] After considering the usual range of responses (wearing a mask, destroying cameras, ironic attention-drawing in the manner of the Surveillance Camera Players), Selvaggio hit on a particularly obfuscating response with a protester's edge: he produced and distributed masks of his face that were accurate enough so that other people wearing them would be tagged as him by Facebook's facial-recognition software.

Selvaggio's description of the project offers a capsule summary of obfuscation: "[R]ather than try to hide or obscure one's face from the camera, these devices allow you to present a different, alternative identity to the camera, my own."

2.18 Manufacturing conflicting evidence: confounding investigation

The Art of Political Murder: Who Killed the Bishop?—Francisco Goldman's account of the investigation into the death of Bishop Juan José Gerardi Conedera—reveals the use of obfuscation to muddy the waters of evidence collection.[35] Bishop Gerardi, who played an enormously important part in defending human rights during Guatemala's civil war of 1960–1996, was murdered in 1998.

As Goldman documented the long and dangerous process of bringing at least a few of those responsible within the Guatemalan military to justice for this murder, he observed that those threatened by the investigation didn't merely plant evidence to conceal their role. Framing someone else would be an obvious tactic, and the planted evidence would be assumed to be false. Rather, they produced *too much* conflicting evidence, too many witnesses and testimonials, too many possible stories. The goal was not to construct an airtight lie, but rather to multiply the possible hypotheses so prolifically that observers would despair of ever arriving at the truth. The circumstances of the bishop's murder produced what Goldman terms an "endlessly exploitable situation," full of leads that led nowhere and mountains of seized evidence, each factual element calling the others into question. "So much could be made and so much would be made to *seem to connect*," Goldman writes, his italics emphasizing the power of the ambiguity.[36]

The thugs in the Guatemalan military and intelligence services had plenty of ways to manage the situation: access to internal political power, to money, and, of course, to violence and the threat of violence. In view of how opaque the situation remains, we do not want to speculate about exact decisions, but the fundamental goal seems reasonably clear. The most immediately significant adversaries—investigators, judges, journalists—could be killed, menaced, bought, or otherwise influenced. The obfuscating evidence and other materials were addressed to the larger community of observers, a pro-liferation of false leads throwing enough time-wasting doubt over every aspect of the investigation that it could call the ongoing work, and any conclusions, into question.

Understanding Obfuscation

3 WHY IS OBFUSCATION NECESSARY?

Where does a wise man hide a leaf? In the forest. But what does he do if there is no forest? ... He grows a forest to hide it in.

G. K. Chesterton, "The Sign of the Broken Sword"

3.1 Obfuscation in brief

Privacy is a complex and even contradictory concept, a word of such broad meanings that in some cases it can become misleading, or almost meaningless. It is expressed in law and policy, in technology, philosophy, and in everyday conversation. It encompasses a space that runs from a dashboard on a website—your privacy settings, managed through drop-down menus and radio buttons—to an overarching argument about the development of human society. Privacy is an outmoded idea, some say, a two-century anomaly of Western industrialization, the interregnum between village life and social media; privacy makes it possible for us to develop as free-thinking, independent individuals; privacy is an expression of bourgeois hypocrisy and bad faith; privacy is the defense of social diversity ... .[1] This doesn't merely show the ways in which the word is used. A moment's reflection makes clear that within these uses are divergent concepts. The house of privacy has many rooms. Some are concerned with the integrity of family life, some with state oppression (now or in the future), some with the utility and value of data, and some with a true inner self that can only emerge in anonymity, and many have intersections and communicating doors.[2] This conceptual diversity carries over into the strategies, practices, technologies, and tactics used to produce, perform, and protect privacy.[3] Elsewhere we have shown how many of these conceptions can be unified under the banner of contextual integrity, but here our concern is with the connections between these concerns, as they are specifically articulated, and with how we can defend ourselves accordingly.[4]

The purpose of this chapter is to describe what obfuscation is and how it fits into the diverse landscape of privacy interests, threats to those interests, and methods used to address those threats. Privacy is a multi-faceted concept, and a wide range of structures, mechanisms, rules, and practices are available to produce it and defend it. If we open up privacy's tool chest, drawer by metaphorical drawer, we find policy and law at the local, national, and global levels;

provably secure technologies, such as cryptography; the disclosure actions and practices of individuals; social systems of confidentiality (for example, those of journalists, priests, doctors, and lawyers); steganographic systems; collective withholding and *omerta* on the part of a community; and more. We find Timothy May's BlackNet, an application of cryptographic technologies to describe a wholly anonymous information marketplace, with untraceable, untaxable transactions, that fosters corporate espionage and the circulation of military secrets and forbidden and classified materials, with the long-term goal of the "collapse of governments."[5] We find legal work building on the Fourth Amendment to the United States Constitution to establish protections for communications networks and social sites, endeavoring to strike a balance between rights of individual citizens and powers of law enforcement. To this diverse kit we will add obfuscation, both as a method in itself and as an approach that can be used within and alongside other methods, depending on the goal. We aim to persuade readers that for some privacy problems obfuscation is a plausible solution, and that for some it is the best solution.

Obfuscation, at its most abstract, is the production of noise modeled on an existing signal in order to make a collection of data more ambiguous, confusing, harder to exploit, more difficult to act on, and therefore less valuable. The word "obfuscation" was chosen for this activity because it connotes obscurity, unintelligibility, and bewilderment and because it helps to distinguish this approach from methods that rely on disappearance or erasure. Obfuscation assumes that the signal can be spotted in some way and adds a plethora of related, similar, and pertinent signals—a crowd which an individual can mix, mingle, and, if only for a short time, hide.

Consider General Sir Arthur St. Clare, the fictional military martyr in G. K. Chesterton's short story "The Sign of the Broken Sword." General St. Clare's men were slaughtered in an ill-considered attack on an enemy camp. Why did the brilliant strategist attempt an obviously flawed attack on his foe's superior position? Chesterton's ecclesiastical detective, Father Brown, answers with a question: "Where does the wise man hide a pebble?" "On the beach," his friend replies.[6] And he hides a leaf in the forest, Brown continues—and if he needs to hide a body, he must produce many dead bodies among which to hide it. To protect his secret, General St. Clare slays one man, then conceals him by the chaos of other dead men, which he creates by commanding a sudden charge on artillery that has the high ground.

Father Brown's rhetorical question was repeated by the Rt. Hon. Lord Justice Jacob in a 2007 patent case:

> Now it might be suggested that it is cheaper to make this sort of mass disclosure than to consider the documents with some care to decide whether they should be disclosed. And at that stage it might be cheaper—just run it all through the photocopier or CD maker—especially since doing so is an allowable cost. But that isn't the point. For it is the downstream costs caused by over-disclosure which so often are so substantial and so pointless. It can even be said, in cases of massive over-disclosure, that there is a real risk that the really important documents will get overlooked—where does a wise man hide a leaf?[7]

From dead soldiers to disclosed documents, we can see that the essence of obfuscation is in getting things overlooked, and adding to the cost, trouble, and difficulty of doing the looking.

Obfuscation can usefully be compared to camouflage. Camouflage is often thought of as a tool for outright disappearance—think of the scene in *The Simpsons* in which Milhouse imagines putting on his camo outfit and melting into the greenery, with only his glasses and smile still visible.[8] In practice, both natural and man-made camouflage work with a variety of techniques and goals, only some of which are used to try to vanish from view entirely; others make use of "disruptive patterns" that hide the edges, outline, orientation, and movement of a shape with fragments and suggestions of other possible shapes. Breaking up the outlines doesn't make a shape disappear entirely, as when a flounder buries itself in sand or an octopus uses its mantle to masquerade as a rock. Rather, for situations in which avoiding observation is impossible—when we move, change positions, or are otherwise exposed—disruptive patterns and disruptive coloration interfere with assessments of things like range, size, speed, and numbers. They make the individual harder to identify and target, and the members of the group more difficult to count. Many early military uses of camouflage were devoted to making large, hard-to-hide things such as artillery emplacements difficult to assess accurately from the air. In situations in which one can't disappear, producing numerous possible targets or vectors of motion can sow confusion and buy valuable time. If obfuscation has an emblematic animal, it is the family of orb-weaving spiders, *Cyclosa mulmeinensis* (mentioned in chapter 2), which fill their webs with decoys of themselves. The decoys are far from perfect copies, but when a wasp strikes they work well enough to give the orb-weaver a second or two to scramble to safety.

Hannah Rose Shell's history of camouflage, *Hide and Seek: Camouflage, Photography, and the Media of Reconnaissance*, develops the theme of "camouflage consciousness," a way of being and acting based on one's internal model of the surveillance technology against which one must work.[9] Shell argues that a camoufleur producing patterns, a specialist training soldiers, and the soldiers on a battlefield were attempting to determine their visibility to binoculars and telescopic rifle sights, to still and film cameras, to airplanes, spotters, and satellites, and to act in ways that mitigated that visibility. This entailed combining research, estimates, modeling, and guesswork to exploit the flaws and limitations of observational technology. Camouflage, whether seeking the complete invisibility of mimicry or the temporary solution of hiding a shape in a mess of other, ambiguous, obfuscating possible shapes, was always a reflection of the capabilities of the technology against which it was developed.

It is the forms of data obfuscation or information obfuscation that concern us here—their technical utility for designers, developers, and activists. Understanding the moral and ethical roles of such forms of obfuscation means understanding the data-acquisition and data-analysis technologies they can challenge and obstruct. It means understanding the threat models, the goals, and the constraints. Obfuscation is a tool among other tools for the construction and the defense of privacy, and like all tools it is honed on the purposes it can serve and the problems it can solve. To lay out the nature of these problems, we introduce the idea of *information asymmetry*.

3.2 Understanding information asymmetry: knowledge and power

At this point, let us recall Donald Rumsfeld's famously convoluted explanation of the calculus of risk in the run-up to the invasion of Iraq: "there are known knowns, which we know we know; known unknowns, which we know we don't know; and unknown unknowns, which we do not know we don't know."[10] As much as this seems like a deliberate logic puzzle, it distinguishes three very different categories of danger. We can see a surveillance camera mounted on a streetlight, or concealed in a dome of mirrored glass on the ceiling of a hallway, and know we are being recorded. We know that we don't know whether the recording is being transmitted only on the site or whether it is being streamed over the Internet to some remote location. We know that we don't know how long the recording will be stored, or who is authorized to view it—just a security guard watching live, or an insurance inspector in the event of a claim, or the police?

There is a much larger category of unknown unknowns about something as seemingly simple as a CCTV recording. We don't know if the footage can be run through facial-recognition or gait-recognition software, for instance, or if the time code can be correlated with a credit-card purchase, or with the license plate of a car we exited, to connect our image with our identity—in fact, unless we are personally involved with privacy activism or security engineering, we don't even know that we don't know that. Confusing as it is, not only is the triple negative in this sentence accurate; it also indicates the layers of uncertainty: we aren't aware that we can't be sure that the video file will not be analyzed with predictive demographic tools in order to identify likely criminals or terrorists for questioning. This isn't even the end of the unknowns, all potentially shaping consequential decisions produced in a dense cloud of our ignorance. And that is merely one CCTV camera, its cable or wireless transmission terminating somewhere, in some hard drive, that may be backed up somewhere else—under what jurisdictions, what terms, what business arrangements? Multiply this by making a credit-card purchase, signing up for an email list, downloading a smartphone app ("This app requires access to your contacts"? "Sure!"), giving a postal code or a birthday or a identification number in response to a reasonable and legitimate request, and on and on through the day and around the world.

It is obvious that information collection takes place in asymmetrical power relationships: we rarely have a choice as to whether or not we are monitored, what is done with any information that is gathered, or what is done to us on the basis of conclusions drawn from that information. If you want to take a train, make a phone call, use a parking garage, or buy some groceries, you are going to be subject to information gathering and you are going to give up some or all control over elements of that information. It is rarely a matter of explicit agreement in a space of complete information and informed choice. You will have to fill out certain forms in order to receive critical resources or to participate in civic life, and you will have to consent to onerous terms of service in order to use software that your job may require. Moreover, the infrastructure, by default, gathers data on you. Obfuscation is related to this problem of asymmetry of power—as the camouflage comparison suggests, it is an approach suited to situations in which we can't easily escape observation but we must move and act—but this problem is only the surface aspect of information collection, what we know we know. A second aspect, the informational or epistemic asymmetry, is a deeper and more pernicious problem, and plays more of a role in shaping obfuscation in defense of privacy.

Brad Templeton, chair of the Electronic Frontier Foundation, has told a story of the danger of "time-traveling robots from the future"[11] that, with more powerful hardware and sophisticated software than we have today, come back in time and subject us to total surveillance; they connect the discrete (and, we thought, discreet) dots of our lives, turning the flow of our private experience into all-too-clear, all-too-human patterns, shining their powerful analytic light into the past's dark corners. Those robots from the future are mercenaries working for anyone wealthy enough to employ them: advertisers, industries, governments, interested parties. We are helpless to stop them as they collate and gather our histories, because, unlike them, we can't travel through time and change our past actions.

Templeton's story isn't science fiction, however. We produce enormous volumes of data every day. Those data stay around indefinitely, and the technology that can correlate them and analyze them keeps improving. Things we once thought were private—if we thought of that at all—become open, visible, and meaningful to new technologies. This is one aspect of the information asymmetry that shapes our practices of privacy and autonomy: we don't know what near-future algorithms, techniques, hardware, and databases will be able to do with our data. There is a constantly advancing front of transition from meaningless to meaningful—from minor life events to things that can change our taxes, our insurance rates, our access to capital, our freedom to move, or whether we are placed on a list.

That is the future unknown, but there are information asymmetries that should concern us in the present too. Information about us is valuable, and it moves around. A company that has collected information about us may connect it with other disparate pools of records (logs of telephone calls, purchase records, personally identifying information, demographic rosters, activity on social networks, geolocative data), and may then package that information and sell it to other companies—or hand it over in response to a governmental request or a subpoena. Even if those who run a company promise to keep the information to themselves, it may become part of the schedule of assets after a bankruptcy and then be acquired or sold off. All the work of correlation and analysis is done with tools and training that, for most of the people they affect, lie beyond anything more than a superficial understanding. The population at large doesn't have access to the other databases, or to the techniques, the training in mathematics and computer science, or the software and hardware that one must have to comprehend what can be done with seemingly trivial details from their lives and activities, and how such details can potentially provide more powerful, more nearly complete, and more revealing analyses than ordinary users could have anticipated— more revealing, in fact, than even the engineers and analysts could have anticipated.

Tal Zarsky, one of the major theorists of data mining, has described a subtle trap in predictive software—yet another, further step in the asymmetry. Predictive systems draw on huge existing datasets to produce predictions of human activity: they will make predictions, accurate or inaccurate, which will be used to make decisions and produce coercive outcomes, and people will be punished or rewarded for things they have not yet done. The discriminatory and manipulative possibilities are clear. However, as Zarsky explains, there is another layer to these concerns: "A non-interpretable process might follow from a data-mining analysis which is not explainable In human language. Here, the software makes its selection decisions based upon multiple variables (even thousands). ... It would be difficult for the government to provide a detailed response when asked why an individual was singled out to receive differentiated treatment by an automated recommendation system. The most the government could say is that this is what the algorithm found based on previous cases."[12]

Developing these ideas further, Solon Barocas reveals how vulnerable we are to data aggregation, analytics, and predictive modeling—now popularly called "big data." Big data methods take information we have willingly shared, or have been compelled to provide, and produce knowledge from inferences that few—least of all we individual data subjects—could have anticipated.[13] It is not simply that a decision is made and enforced. We can't even be entirely sure that we know *why* a decision is made and enforced, because, in the ultimate unknowable unknown of data collection, those who make the decision don't know why it is made and enforced. We are reduced to guessing at the inner workings of an opaque operation. We do not understand the grounds for judgment. We are in a state of informational asymmetry.

Insofar as this is an argument built partially on what we don't—indeed can't—know, it runs the risk of being a little abstract. But we can make it thoroughly concrete, and discuss a different facet of the problem of information asymmetry, by turning briefly to the subject of risk. Think of "risk" as in "credit risk." As Josh Lauer's research has shown, the management of credit was crucial in the history of data collection, dossier production, and data mining.[14] Transformations in the mercantile and social order of the United States in the nineteenth century obliged businesses to issue credit to customers without having access to the "personal acquaintance and community opinion" that formerly had figured in calculations of trust and risk. In the place of "personal acquaintance and community opinion," they relied on credit bureaus to collect data that could be used to make informed decisions as to whether individuals would receive loans, insurance, leases, and other risky things. By the late 1920s, credit bureaus' reports and analyses constituted a private surveillance system on a scale that dwarfed any domestic project conducted by the U.S. government. Several major consequences followed from this, among them the coercion of character assessment built into one's "financial identity" and the rise of targeted marketing as new uses for the accumulated data were invented. One consequence is particularly relevant to our argument here. That consequence, which really comes into play with the rise of digital databases and tools, is that credit reporting decreases risk, yes, but under some circumstances it also *exports* risk. (These consequences are in the domain of Anthony Giddens's "manufactured risks": dangers produced by the process of modernization, rather than mitigated by it, and, in turn, requiring new systems of mitigation.[15])

In the process of decreasing risk for a lender, an insurance company, or a business opening a line of credit for a customer, risks are increased for the individual. One risk is that of identity theft: you have to trust a department store's subcontractor, whoever that is, to follow immaculate security practices. Another is the risk of violations of context, such as the store's selling data to shady data brokers, sharing data with partners, letting data be acquired with the rest of a company, or letting data be gathered indiscriminately by government in the course of some larger data-collection project. This may be a fair trade, but it is important to remember that risk doesn't disappear with data collection—new forms of risk are created and externalized by those who hold the data. Those risks will be borne by you, and by others whom your data can be used to better analyze and understand. On a larger scale, the surveillance and data-collection projects our governments launch in the name of security are always about protection from one class of risks against which the state must defend, but they produce another class of risks whose danger citizens take on: the risk that dissent will be stifled, the risk that legitimate opposition will be crushed, or just the risk that accidents will happen and innocent people will be detained, tracked, exposed, and punished. These are cases in which increasing the volume and the detail of information collected reduces risk for some while increasing it for others—an experience of information asymmetry we encounter every day and believe certain forms of obfuscation can help to correct.

"They" (or a range of "they"s) know much about us, and we know little about them or about what they can do. Situations so asymmetrical in knowledge, power, and risk make effective responses difficult to plan, much less carry out. These are not the asymmetries of the priest or the busybody in a small town where people know one another's business and some people know more than others. What we describe here is different because of the convergence of asymmetries: those who know about us have power over us. They can deny us employment, deprive us of credit, restrict our movements, refuse us shelter, membership, or education, and limit our access to the good life.

3.3 The fantasy of opting out

Of course, we still *choose* to participate in these asymmetrical relationships, don't we? For most of these forms of data collection, some of the fault must lie with the individuals who use services or engage with institutions that offer unfavorable terms of service and are known to misbehave. Isn't putting all the blame on government institutions and private services unfair, when they are trying to maintain security and capture some of the valuable data produced by their users? Doesn't this subject the users to classic moral hazard, making service providers take on the burden of risk and responsibility for choices that users make? Can't we users just opt out of systems with which we disagree?

To see to what degree simply opting out is increasingly unreasonable, consider a day in the life of a fairly ordinary person in a large city in a stable, democratically governed country. She is not in prison or institutionalized, nor is she a dissident or an enemy of the state, yet she lives in a condition of permanent and total surveillance unprecedented in its precision and intimacy. As soon as she leaves her apartment, she is on camera: while in the hallway and the elevator of her building, when using the ATM outside her bank (which produces a close-up image time-stamped with her withdrawal record), while passing shops and waiting at crosswalks, while in the subway station and on the train, while in the lobby, the elevator, and her cubicle in her workplace—and all that before lunch. A montage of very nearly every move of her life in the city outside her apartment could be assembled, and each step accounted for—particularly if she chooses to don her fitness-tracking device. But that montage would hardly be necessary: her mobile phone, in the course of its ordinary operation of seeking base stations and antennas to keep her connected as she walks, provides a constant log of her position and movements. Any time she spends in "dead zones" without phone reception can also be accounted for: her subway pass logs her entry into the subway, and her radio-frequency identification badge produces a record of her entry into the building in which she works. (If she drives a car, her electronic toll-collection pass serves a similar purpose, as does automatic license-plate imaging.) If her apartment is part of a smart-grid program, spikes in her electricity usage can reveal exactly when she is up and around, turning on lights and ventilation fans and using the microwave oven and the coffee maker.

Before we return to the question of opting out, consider how thoroughly the systems mentioned in the preceding paragraph are embedded in our hypothetical ordinary person's everyday life, far more invasively than mere logs of her daily comings and goings. Someone observing her could assemble in forensic detail her social and familial connections, her struggles and interests, and her beliefs and commitments. From Amazon purchases and Kindle highlights, from purchase records linked with her loyalty cards at the drugstore and the supermarket, from Gmail metadata and chat logs, from search-history and checkout records from the public library, from Netflix-streamed movies, and from activity on Facebook and Twitter, dating sites, and other social networks, a very specific and personal narrative is clear. The mobile device in her pocket, the fitness-tracking device around her wrist, and the Event Data

Recorder installed in her car follow her when she is on the move. When even some of the data are pooled and correlated with data produced by others like her, powerful demographic inferences and predictions can be made. We know our subject with a thoroughness that would be the envy of any secret-police agent of a few decades ago—and with relatively little effort, as our subject spies on herself for us.

If the apparatus of total surveillance that we have described here were deliberate, centralized, and explicit, a Big Brother machine toggling between cameras, it would demand revolt, and we could conceive of a life outside the totalitarian microscope. But if we are nearly as observed and documented as any person in history, our situation is a prison that, although it has no walls, bars, or wardens, is difficult to escape.

Which brings us back to the problem of "opting out." For all the dramatic language about prisons and panopticons, the sorts of data collection we describe here—the kinds to which obfuscation is a response—are, in democratic countries, still theoretically voluntary. But the costs of refusal are high and getting higher: a life lived in ramifying social isolation, using any pay phones you can find (there are half as many in New York City as there were just five years ago) or mobile "burners," able to accept only very particular forms of employment, living far from centers of business and commerce, without access to many forms of credit, insurance, or other significant financial instruments, not to mention the minor inconveniences and disadvantages—long waits at road toll cash lines, higher prices at grocery stores, inferior seating on airline flights—for which disclosure is the unspecified price.[16] It isn't possible for everyone to live on principle; as a practical matter, many of us must make compromises in asymmetrical relationships, without the control or consent for which we might wish. In those situations—everyday twenty-first-century life—there are still ways to carve out spaces of resistance, counterargument, and autonomy. They are weapons of the weak.

3.4 Weapons of the weak: what obfuscation can do

The political scientist James C. Scott went to "Sedaka," a pseudonymized village in Malaysia, to answer a question that has engaged historians, anthropologists, and activists of all stripes: How do people who lack the commonly recognized means of political recourse—votes, money, violence—engage in resistance?[17] Peasants, sharecroppers, and corvée laborers have their work captured and surplus extracted from it, whether as grain, cash, various forms of debt, or time in uncompensated occupations. Only rarely can the peasants risk a confrontation with the forces that take advantage of them. They have fewer resources on which to draw, in order to make dramatic and historically memorable stands against injustice, than skilled industrial workers in urban centers have. Scott was interested in an empirical question: What do peasants, in the face of obviously unjust actions, *do*? The answer was a list of ordinary, everyday, eminently practical ways of taking action and talking back, which Scott gathered under the heading "weapons of the weak." These join the rich and varied accounts of resisting and keeping some measure of autonomy in the balance between consent and outright refusal—most notably, in regard to surveillance, in the work of Gary Marx.[18]

It is obvious, but still worth saying, that we do not intend a one-to-one comparison between the people chronicled by Scott and, generally, the users of obfuscation. Nor do we see obfuscation as having precisely the same set of limitations and properties as Scott's concept. For purposes of this book, we are inspired by fundamental themes in Scott's idea: we can better understand acts of obfuscation within a context of unavoidable relationships between people and institutions with large informational and power asymmetries. To begin, we observe the necessarily small and additive nature of many of these "weapons"—obfuscation and the ones Scott observes—reflecting their role in an ongoing and open-ended set of social and political arrangements, rather than an overturning world revolution. Instead of a mass invasion of inequitably distributed land, the approach is to squat or poach. Pilfering and thumb-on-the-scale fraud (the phenomenon large retailers euphemistically call "merchandise shrinkage") are fractional versions of the project of the re- allocation of needful things. The response to orders is not some cinematic refusal, but foot dragging, slowdowns, feigned ignorance, deliberate stupidity, and the pretense of compliance. Finally, and most important for our purposes, rather than overt backtalk or heroic here-we-stand speeches there is the evasive muttering, gossip, and slander of what Scott terms the *hidden transcript*.[19]

It is likely that every reader of this book has turned away from a superior (occupational, filial, legal, religious, or otherwise) and subvocally muttered dissent. Perhaps the dissent takes place wholly in the mind; perhaps one dares a barely audible murmur, meant for oneself alone; perhaps it is shared in privacy among subordinate groups. (As Scott points out, powerful groups also have hidden transcripts—ways of accumulating and maintaining power that can't be generally discussed or disclosed.) Dissent in a workplace may take the form of gossip, jokes, anecdotes, or stories that make it possible to criticize the order of power without speaking outright. Dissent creates a space in which the dignity and relative autonomy of the speaker can exist, even as it accomplishes other things. An assertion is made, however covertly, that one is not what one may publicly appear to be.

With that outline in place, we will lay out a few quick distinctions. No reasonable analogy can be made between one of the peasants Scott studied and an obfuscator who is installing a browser extension or running a Tor relay; the breadth of resources available to one and the other—the structures and infrastructures—and the mechanisms of coercion and control they face do not allow for simple comparisons. As our summary here suggests, though, part of what Scott accomplishes is *broadening the spectrum of responses* to oppression and coercion that we take into account. It's not just armed uprising or nothing at all, and no one is merely passive. There are very different degrees of access to the power, wealth, status, and other components of autonomy and redress, but we push back when and where we can. Taking up this thread, we can look to one of the perennial questions about digital privacy: Why don't people use powerful, verifiably reliable, openly audited, robust protection systems, such as end-to-end public-key encryption of their messages—"strong" cryptography? Why not use the optimal system?

We do not want to argue that they shouldn't. Quite the opposite! There are, however, times, circumstances, populations, and events in which the strong system, the optimal system, isn't possible, accessible, desirable, or some combination of the three. Situations arise in which we are obligated to be visible, in which we *need* to be visible, or *want* to be visible (whether to friends or compatriots, or as an act of public protest or presence) and still we want to muddy our tracks as best we can. Sometimes we don't have a choice about having our data collected, so we may as well (if we feel strongly about it) put a little sand in the gears. When doing work for government or when developing software, we may have to gather data to provide service, but still seek to do right by our users and to protect their interests from future groups who don't share our good intentions. In those moments, under those constraints, we often are stuck with weaker systems, or strong systems with a few weak components, and are, ourselves, "weak."

We want to follow Scott but take his work in a slightly different direction as we broaden the spectrum of responses to situations involving data surveillance and obfuscation. There is real *utility* in an obfuscation approach, whether that utility lies in bolstering an existing strong privacy system, in covering up some specific action, in making things marginally harder for an adversary, or even in the "mere gesture" of registering our discontent and refusal. An obfuscation approach offers expressive and functional—though sometimes fragile—methods of protest and evasion that are accessible to a range of actors but are particularly important for actors who lack access to other methods or wish to complement them. Thus we apply the concept of "weapons of the weak."

Before we turn, in the next section, to the kinds of situations in which obfuscation may be useful, one more bit of explanation is necessary to avoid confusion: "Strong" forces can, and do, use obfuscation techniques. Consider some of the examples cited in the book thus far: corporate over-disclosure of documents in legal cases, anticompetitive tricks by companies, the manufacturing of evidence, and some military camouflage technologies. The weak *need* to be invisible, to escape notice, but being invisible can also be advantageous to the strong. Our argument is one of relative utility. Let's put this bluntly: If you have access to wealth, the law, social sanction, and force, if you have the whole vocabulary of *strong systems* at your disposal, on the advantageous side of the asymmetry of power, and can retain top lawyers and hire sharp programmers, why bother with obfuscation? If you have diplomatic pouches and NSA-secured phone lines, you need not waste your time shuffling SIM cards and making up identities. Obfuscation does sometimes come in handy for powerful actors with strong systems for privacy already in place, and we discuss that aspect accordingly, but it is a tool more readily adopted by those stuck with a weak system.

3.5 Distinguishing obfuscation from strong privacy systems

So far, we have contended that there are times when optimal, "strong" security and privacy practices aren't practical or available for individuals and groups. This is not an argument against other systems and practices; it is merely an acknowledgment that there are circumstances in which obfuscation may provide an appropriate alternative or could be added to an existing technology or approach. Obfuscation can serve a function akin to the hidden transcript, concealing dissent and covert speech and providing an opportunity to assert one's sense of autonomy—an act of refusal concealed within a gesture of assent—or can provide more straightforward tools for protest or obscurity. There are situations in which many people may periodically find themselves obligated to give things up, with uncertain consequences and without a clear mechanism for reasserting control—moments when obfuscation can play a role, providing not a comprehensive military-grade data-control solution (though it may be usefully combined with such a solution) but an intuitive approach to throwing up a bit of smoke.

Explaining what obfuscation is requires us to clarify what it is not and what empty spaces it fills (as Scott's "weapons of the weak" fill the space between consent and insurrection). It requires us to discuss what obfuscation accomplishes that other services and systems don't accomplish, and what it costs in difficulty, wasted data, and wasted time. In the context of data protection via optimal technology, business best practice, or legislation and governmental intervention, what makes obfuscation necessary? In view of the costs obfuscation can impose, why should one turn to it? Describing these costs, and making our argument in light of them, will clarify obfuscation in general before we frame it in terms of the ethical and political concerns (in chapter 4) and then in terms of designing for specific goals and outcomes (in chapter 5).

We have already addressed one of the alternatives from which obfuscation must distinguish itself: individuals' opting out of any platform, service, or interaction that would misuse their data. This is a solution that seems to be free of moral compromise—they disagree and therefore decline, causing no trouble. Though such opting out may be possible for a very narrow range of possible users and uses, it isn't a practical or reasonable choice for all. Martyrdom is rarely a productive choice in a political calculus; as straightforward as the rational-actor binary of opting in or out may be, a choice between acceptance and dropping off the edge of the (networked) earth isn't really a choice at all. We often end up in compromised situations, trying to make the best decision from a narrow menu of options that are problematic to various degrees and in various ways. The user who makes consistently perfect choices about data security and privacy is, like the perfectly rational economic agent, more likely to be found in theory than in practice, and in practice such a person would be a strange balance between a technologist of great sophistication and a Luddite refusenik.

What about relying on businesses to adopt best practices for their customers?

Of course, the users are not the only part of the data-acquisition equation. The companies involved could resolve many of the concerns users have, rendering obfuscation moot. A well-designed opt-out policy could offer fine-tuned control of the processes of aggregation and analysis, allowing you to make choices that lay between the extremes of refusal and compliance. It would enable one to receive certain benefits in return for a degree of use, and it would specify that data could be gathered or deployed only in certain contexts, only for certain purposes, and for only a set period of time. That might offer genuine options for users to evaluate. However, private-sector efforts of this kind are hampered by the fact that companies, for good reasons and bad, are the major strategic beneficiaries of data mining. The present-day consumer economy runs on data—surveys, conversion analysis, customer-retention analysis, demography, targeted advertising, and data collected at the point of sale that feed back through the entire supply chain, from the just-in-time production facility to the trend-spotting system.[20] Whether the particular company in question is in the business of gathering, bundling, and selling individual data (as DoubleClick and Acxiom are), whether it has used data generated and provided by its customers to improve its operations (as Amazon and Wal-Mart have), whether it is based on user-data-driven advertising revenue (as Google is), or whether it subcontracts the analysis of consumer data for purposes of spotting credit, insurance, or rental risks, it isn't in a company's interest to support general restraints on access to this information.[21]

Owing to the competitive disadvantage associated with general restraints on access to information, any individual company risks losing the returns on data about customers, clients, consumers, even patients. Web publishers—particularly those who must answer to shareholders—are terrified to leave the value that can be derived from personal information "on the table," unexploited. Further, the liquidity and portability of data renders any piecemeal strategy of relinquishment highly problematic, because material of little consequence when in the hands of one company can result in a serious breach of privacy when in the hands of another company that has access to a richer or better-managed database. For companies in the information services industry, or companies utilizing data to promote their competitive edge, consumers' chagrin and occasional fines and slaps on the wrist are a small enough cost of doing business, and such companies fight fiercely to retain access to the "standing reserve" of personal data.[22]

What about relying on government to enact and enforce better laws?

Isn't government supposed to be the venue where interests are balanced and values and political principles protected? This raises another question against which obfuscation must justify itself: Why are businesses having to invent data-collection and data-management practices on their own? Surely such practices should be defined and enforced by governments.

Indeed, regulation and law have historically been central bulwarks of personal privacy, from the Fourth Amendment of the U.S. Constitution to the European Union's data-protection requirements and directives. Our laws probably will be the eventual site of the conversation in which we answer, as a society, hard questions about the harvesting and stockpiling of personal information. But they operate slowly, and whatever momentum propels agents of government and law in the direction of protecting privacy in the public interest it is amply counterbalanced by opposing forces of corporations and other institutional actors, including government itself.

In the world after Snowden, it has become clear that, for many national-security, espionage, and law-enforcement organizations, having a population already predisposed to disclose to companies huge volumes of information about themselves that can either be subpoenaed or covertly exploited is all to the good.[23] Poorly designed and managed social platforms create an efficiently self-spying population, doing their own wiretapping gratis with photos uploaded with their EXIF metadata intact and with detailed social chit-chat waiting to be subjected to data-mining algorithms.

Particularly in the United States, people will have to ask careful and demanding questions about any governmental project to reform data-collection rules and practices. Enormous quantities of personal data are already in circulation. Ever-increasing amounts of freely provided personal data are packaged and sold, while the patient and uncertain work of legislation and judicial decision unfolds slowly, with some forward steps and some backward steps. The rate of progress doesn't inspire great optimism. This brings us back to the question with which we began: Since technologies have generated the context and the parameters of many of these problems, why can't superior technologies solve them?

What about relying on superior technological solutions?

Powerful, thoughtful, well-designed systems have been produced to preserve and enhance privacy, be it in data mining, surfing or searching the Web, or transmitting confidential information. Yet the situation remains imperfect. Producing tools for detecting data provenance, properly anonymizing datasets, generating contextual awareness, and providing secure, confidential communication poses serious technical challenges. Potential systems like these also face resistance from well-heeled business interests and governmental organizations that would rather we used inferior, badly implemented, and poorly adopted (and adapted) systems.[24] Furthermore, no matter how convincing the technical developments and standards, adoption by societal actors whose organizations and institutions mediate many flows of data is fraught with politics. Even on the individual scale, difficulties persist, as Arvind Narayanan notes in his study of the use of "Pragmatic Crypto" (as distinct from "Cypherpunk Crypto," a techno-determinist project to wholly reshape society through encryption)—adoption is fraught with complex engineering and usability issues for the developers.[25] None of these problems diminish the accomplishments or the utility of privacy technologies, from Tor to Off-the-Record (OTR) messaging to email encryption toolkits such as Gnu Privacy Guard (GPG). Yet the combination of technical accomplishments, law and regulation, industry best practice, and user choice leaves great, neglected, unprotected empty spaces, like a Venn diagram in negative, in which obfuscation comes into its own.

As we will discuss later in more practical detail, obfuscation is, in part, a *troublemaking* strategy. Although privacy is served by the constraints of law and regulation, disclosure limits imposed by organizational best practices, protective technological affordances provided by conscientious developers, and the exercise of abstinence or opting out, the areas of vulnerability remain vast. Obfuscation promises an additional layer of cover for these. Obfuscation obscures by making noise and muddying the waters; it can be used for data disobedience under difficult circumstances and as a digital weapon for the informationally weak.

Be fire with fire; Threaten the threatener and outface the brow.
Shakespeare, *King John*, 1595

After a lecture on TrackMeNot,[1] a member of the audience rose to say that she was deeply troubled by the valorization of deceit and dishonesty. To her it didn't seem right to submit search queries that were not of true interest. The question of deception has not been the sole source of opposition to obfuscation; other sources of opposition include wastefulness, free riding, database pollution, and violation of terms of service.

Challenges such as that made by the woman at the lecture were worrisome to us: ours was supposed to be the moral high ground, with TrackMeNot defending individuals against illegitimate and exploitative information practices. But such challenges could not be summarily brushed aside. Because obfuscating tactics are often fundamentally adversarial, involving dissimulation and misdirection, the appropriation of resources for unintended or undesired uses must be explained and justified. In an article titled "A Tack in the Shoe," Gary Marx writes: "Criteria are needed which would permit us to speak of 'good' and 'bad,' or appropriate and inappropriate efforts to neutralize the collection of personal data."[2] To use obfuscation because it works, or even because it is the only approach that works, isn't enough. Obfuscation, if used, must be defensible on ethical grounds, and must be compatible with the political values of the society in which one lives.

TrackMeNot exposed many of the ethical issues that can confront not only developers of obfuscating systems but also users, and as a consequence exposed a need to distinguish uses that are morally defensible from uses that are not. Intuition places the Craigslist robber, with his unwilling identically dressed confederates, among the latter, and the Allies' radar chaff among the former, but why? What makes them different? And how might we adapt the answer to more ambiguous cases? Mere approval or disapproval isn't sufficient if we are to defend the legitimacy of a particular system; instead, we must provide systematic reasons why that system avoids moral and political hazards.

This chapter prepares designers or users of obfuscation to meet a range of challenges they are likely to confront. Some of the challenges are ethical, claiming that obfuscation causes harm or violates ethical rights beyond general harms. Other challenges are political, suggesting that obfuscation abridges political rights and values, that it is unfair or unjust, that it redistributes power in illegitimate ways, or that it is generally at odds with the political values of surrounding societies or communities.

4.1 Ethics of obfuscation

Dishonesty

It is nearly impossible to avoid charges of dishonesty when the aim of obfuscation is to mislead and misdirect. Linking obfuscation to the ethics of lying leads to a vast landscape of philosophical thought that, though beyond the scope of our book, contributes important insights to our more limited purpose.

The classic Kantian position on lying, which holds that it is absolutely wrong and which famously prescribes truth even in reply to a murderer seeking to locate an innocent victim, would condemn any use of obfuscation. Other defenses of lying have been based on more varied and more contingent ethical positions. Generally, the literature on lying has two strands, one concerned with defining lying and the other with its ethics—whether it is always wrong, whether it is ever right, and whether, even if wrong, it ever can be excused. In practice these two strands are interdependent, because a hard line on the wrongness of lying is softened by a narrow definition. Thomas Aquinas, for example, allowed prudent dissimulation to pass the ethical test not because lying is sometimes morally acceptable but because dissimulation sometimes falls outside of the definition.[3] Our guess is that few people are as resolutely committed to truth-telling as Kant and Aquinas, and that most would condone lying with appropriate justification, such as preventing egregious harm, acting under duress, keeping a promise, or achieving other important ends.[4]

In many of the cases we have discussed in this book, obfuscation presents a means of resisting coercion, exploitation, or threat—ends that might generally legitimize acts of dishonesty. We might say, therefore, that whether obfuscation, like lying, is morally defensible depends on the legitimacy of its ends: radar chaff protecting Allied bombers passes the test, but disseminating malware, robbing a bank, or fixing an election does not, even though we might admire or chuckle at the ingenuity of those who do such things. We do not want to overstate the conclusion and say that legitimate ends alone justify obfuscation, insofar as it is a form of dishonesty; we want to say only that legitimate ends are a necessary condition for ethical obfuscation.

Even in the case that someone chooses obfuscation to achieve praiseworthy he or she will need to defend this choice against further challenges. After we have explored some of the other ethical charges aimed against obfuscation, we will return to the question of sufficiency in order to explain what still is missing from an ethical assessment beyond laudable or even simply acceptable ends.

Waste

Critics may say that an obfuscation system is wasteful if it draws on any important resources to generate noise. In the case of TrackMeNot, for example, some complained about its wasteful use of search engines' servers, its burden on network bandwidth and even its unnecessary draw on electricity. Similarly, CacheCloak[5] could be faulted for wasting network and mobile-app resources, many noise-generating social-network tools for drawing excessively on Facebook's services, and Uber for squandering the effort of drivers responding to spurious calls. In defense of one's preferred obfuscation system, one should immediately recognize a hidden agenda in any such accusations, for the notion of waste is thoroughly normative. It presumes standards of acceptable, desirable, or legitimate use, consumption, exploitation, or employment of the resources in question. Only a strong societal consensus around these standards elevates such charges above mere personal opinion, and only a sound foundation in factual knowledge lends credibility to the suggestion that any particular obfuscation system wastes resources.

When standards are not settled, however, there is greater uncertainty over the line between use and waste. We might all agree that carelessly leaving a tap running is a waste of water, but residents of Los Angeles disagree with residents of Seattle over whether daily watering to maintain verdant lawns in a desert climate is wasteful. To defend TrackMeNot against charges of wastefulness, we can point out that its network usage is minimal compared with usage generated by image, audio, and video files, rich information flows on social networks, and Internet-based communications services. Yet noting huge differences in scale between the traffic generated by TrackMeNot search terms and those needed to maintain (say) Bitcoin or *World of Warcraft* doesn't address the complaint fully. After all, the cumulative flow of a dripping faucet may be far less than the amount of water a daily shower requires, but the former may still be judged wasteful because it is unnecessary.

Whether one considers the noise produced by systems such as Cache-Cloak and TrackMeNot wasteful depends not only on the volume of the noise but also on one's values. A defender points out that protecting privacy by preventing profiling on the basis of search queries is worth the bandwidth—certainly more worthwhile than a good number of the videos clogging bandwidth en route from servers to households. Some critics remain doubtful, though their doubts are less about wasteful usage of common resources than about waste of private ones, such as the server space belonging to providers of search engines and mobile apps. Here too, both quantity and legitimacy matter. In cases where noise overloads an adversary's system or, in more extreme cases, even consumes all available resources, it becomes a denial-of-service attack and the bar of justification is very high. Unless you can convincingly demonstrate that your target is engaged in oppressive, domineering, or clearly unfair practices, a debilitating obfuscation attack is difficult to justify.

In the case where an obfuscating system merely uses but does not debilitate a privately owned resource, what counts as legitimate may not be obvious. Take the case of Web searching. Manually submitted queries, no matter how frivolous the purpose, seem not to provoke complaints of waste. No one argues that "ninja turtle" or "fantasy football" is more wasteful of Google's server resources than, say, "symptoms of Ebola," although some critics have said that the automated search queries submitted by TrackMeNot are wasteful. We can think of no other reason for such criticism than that TrackMeNot's queries run counter to Google's interests, desires, or preferences and that *these*, according to critics, trump users' interests, desires, or preferences for privacy-seeking obfuscation. Such is the rhetorical struggle between those who defend obfuscation as a means of protecting its users against illegitimate information capture, and those who are targets of obfuscation who label such actions wasteful. The winner of this debate captures the ethical high ground and transforms a private dispute over conflicting vested interests into a matter of public morality. But it is important to see, in this instance, that when defenders of search resources vilify obfuscation as "waste," they beg the very question that we, collectively, have not yet properly addressed. In the name of privacy protection, query obfuscation utilizes private resources without owners' authorization, but whether we deem this wasteful or legitimate, prohibited or allowed, is a political question about the exercise of power and privilege and a question to which we will return later in the chapter.

Free riding

Depending on the design of one's preferred obfuscation system, one may be accused of free riding—that is, taking advantage of other people's willingness to submit to the collection, aggregation, and analysis of data or of using services provided by data collectors while denying them profit from your personal information. In the first instance, the adversary will go after the less costly target—people who don't obfuscate—just as predators, according to the adage, go after the slower prey. In the second instance, if you use services offered by targets such as Facebook and Foursquare in ways that diverge from the terms of service, you are violating an implied contract and are free riding not only on people whose behaviors comply with the terms of service but also on investments made by the providers of the services. This applies, for instance, to users of ad-blocking browser plug-ins, who can enjoy a quieter, faster-loading, ad-free Web experience while having access to content underwritten by users who haven't installed ad blockers. Or so the critics suggest. Cast as free riders, obfuscators appear to be sneaks more than rebels; after all, when you aspire to the moral high ground, do you want instead to be someone who games the system by exploiting the ignorance and foolishness of others? These charges must be taken seriously, but in our view whether they stick depends on answers to two questions: Is your obfuscation system (either one you have created or one you are using) freely available to others? And are people who aren't obfuscating left no worse off as a result of your use of that system? When the answers to both of those questions are Yes, as holds for many of the systems we have discussed, we see no exploitation, no moral wrong. When the answer to either question is No, the situation is complex and requires further probing. Secretive obfuscation may be excusable if it leaves non-obfuscators no worse off; obfuscation that disadvantages non-obfuscators may be justified if it is widely and freely available to all. Though further justification is needed in both scenarios, the case that poses the most difficult questions is closed, secretive obfuscation that results in disadvantage to non-obfuscators.

These difficult questions plunge us into philosophical debates about moral responsibility. Even in the worst case, you might redirect blame to the targets of your obfuscating system: the data gatherers. You may ask "Who is taking advantage of whom?" Returning to the metaphor of predator and prey, you can argue "Don't blame me for being fleet footed; it is the predator, after all, who is responsible for the demise of its victims." Though you expose your slower compatriots to higher odds of capture, surely blame accrues primarily to the predator. This leaves a stalemate of mutual recrimination, the data collector accusing the obfuscator of free riding on services and the obfuscator accusing the data collector of free riding on personal information.

In the dominant economy of the Internet, individual users enjoy free services, which are sustained by the value extracted from information about those users by ad networks and by other third-party data aggregators. Unlike traditional commercial market-based exchanges, where a price is explicitly paid for goods or services, the economy into which the Internet has settled is based on the capture of information by indirect, subtle, and often well-hidden means. The informational price—effectively a blank check—is anything but free, according to experts whose commentaries have inspired our own thoughts on this matter.[6] When relinquishment of personal information with no reasonable account of its use is a necessary condition for receiving a service, when it is disproportionate to need (as in over-collection), and when it is inappropriate (as when it violates contextual expectations), such a price is exploitative and the practice is oppressive. Furthermore, when traditional institutional protections aren't effective in addressing practices such as these, the obfuscator who has been accused of free riding may justly challenge the presumptive entitlements of the entrenched system, in which naive users succumb to rhetorical trickery that engages them in terms of exchange they have had little hand in setting.[7] Each party has an interest in setting terms for the exchange of valuable resources, but which interests are favored must be fairly settled or, says the obfuscator, this is a claim that doesn't warrant respect.

This argument doesn't make all information obfuscation legitimate and defensible against the charge of free riding; it does so only when other moral requirements are met and the question of free riding hinges on who is entitled to surplus value generated by the interactions of individual users with service providers collecting information on them. In other words, after you have satisfied yourself that your system meets other ethical criteria, such as worthy ends, questions that remain about conflicting interests and desires or about fair distribution of benefits and entitlements enter the realms of economic and political analysis, taken up below.

Pollution, subversion, and system damage

The charge of data pollution is as vexing as it is unavoidable. Obfuscation, defined as the insertion of noise, invites a parallel to pollution—making something impure or unclean. Someone who taints water, soil, or air with toxic chemicals, particulates, or waste can be roundly criticized because environmental integrity is highly valued not only as an ideal but also as a practical goal. However, critics drawing on the normative clout of environmental pollution aren't coolly observing that obfuscation clutters a data repository; they are alleging that it contaminates a data environment whose integrity is prized. There is, however, a difference. In most present-day societies, the value of the natural environment is presumed and an action that has been shown to pollute it is considered reprehensible. But unless one can make an explicit case that a data assemblage is worthy of protection, a claim for its integrity begs the question.

Even environmental integrity isn't absolutely valued and has been traded off against other values, such as security, commerce, and property rights. Analogously, in order for a charge of data pollution to stick, a data assemblage must be shown to hold greater value than whatever the obfuscator aims to protect. Simply revealing negative consequences for a database is, once again, to beg the ethical question. It comes down to this: Data pollution is unethical only when the integrity of the data flow or data set in question is ethically required. Moreover, whether the integrity of the data outweighs other values and interests at stake must be explicitly settled. When what is in question is whether the interests of a data collector are negatively affected by obfuscation, ethical questions can be settled only by establishing that these interests are of general value and that they override the interests of the obfuscator. When there are no clear moral grounds favoring the respective, conflicting interests (or preferences) of a data collector and an obfuscator, a political resolution, or perhaps a market-based resolution, may be the best one can hope for.

If there *is* genuine public interest in the integrity of particular data flows or data sets, and if obfuscation negatively affects the system as a whole, the burden shifts to the obfuscator to justify his or her actions. For example, one may justly challenge the obfuscator who diminishes the integrity of a population health database when so doing reduces the potential public benefits it can provide. But even in a case such as this, we should assess whether the price an individual pays for the benefit of others or in the public interest is fair. If individuals are coerced to contribute, it should be with assurances that how the information will be used, where it will travel, and how it will be secured will, at the very least, be in line with familiar principles of fair information practice. In other words, the ethical argument hinges on two considerations: whether the data in question are of genuine public and common interest and how much individuals are asked to sacrifice on behalf of such interests. Keeping both of these considerations in sight recognizes that the integrity of a data assemblage—even one deemed valuable—is not absolute, and data controllers have the burden of defending the public importance of the assemblage (and associated practices) as well as the legitimacy of any burdens it might impose on individual data subjects.

In the discussion thus far, we have not differentiated among the three terms "pollution," "subversion," and "system damage." You might want to consider which of the three is relevant when striving to ensure an ethically defensible system. Obfuscating systems that pollute or subvert only the obfuscators' data trail pose fewer ethical challenges than those that also affect other data subjects, and even fewer than those that interfere with a system's general functioning, as in a denial of service. A careful assessment would involve asking questions similar to those we have discussed above— questions concerning respective harms, entitlements, societal welfare and proportionality—about data collection as well as about data obfuscation in relation to legitimate ends.

4.2 From ethics to politics

Ends and means

Since obfuscation almost always involves dissemblance, unauthorized uses of system resources, or impairment of functionality, appreciating obfuscation's intended ends, aims, purposes, or goals, is crucial to evaluating its moral standing. Although some ends might seem unequivocally good and others unequivocally bad, a vast middle ground exists that encompasses merely unproblematic ends (e.g., foiling supermarket surveillance) and ends that are somewhat controversial (e.g., enabling peer-to-peer file sharing). In these zones of ethical ambiguity or flexibility, politics and policy come into play.

Ends, however, are only part of the picture—necessary but not sufficient conditions. Ethical theory and common sense demand that means, too, be defensible, and, as the saying warns, ends may not justify all means. Whether means are acceptable may rest on numerous ethical factors but, as often, may depend on the interaction of ends with various contingent and contextual factors, whose consideration resides in the zone of the political.

Recognizing that certain disputes over ethical issues are best resolved politically doesn't necessarily remove them from ethical consideration entirely when one takes a view, such as Isaiah Berlin's, of political philosophy as moral inquiry, "applied to groups and nations, and indeed, mankind as a whole."[8] In some instances, disagreements over the ethics of obfuscation that reduce to disagreements over clashing ends and values may yet be amenable to purely ethical resolutions, such as the resolution Kant seems to have found when he prioritized truth over preventing murder. But disagreements over ends may not always be accessible to purely ethical reasoning. In these cases, resolution becomes a matter for social policy because how these disagreements are settled affects the constitution or shape of the society in which they are embedded. Ethical questions such as those requiring societal resolution have inspired political philosophers through the ages—from Plato to Hobbes and Rousseau to the present—who have sought to compare and evaluate political systems, to identify political properties and modes of decision making that characterize good societies, and to articulate political principles of justice, fairness, and decency. When we conclude that answers to ethical questions must be answered politically, because they are about the distribution of power, authority, and goods in society, we still have ethics on our minds. We do not mean *any* society; we mean societies opposed to tyranny and striving to be good, just, and decent in the ways that great philosophers, critical thinkers, and political leaders have idealized in word and action. With this in mind, let us revisit the issues of dishonesty (dissimulation), waste, free riding, pollution, and system damage arising in the context of obfuscation.

As we worked through the issue of waste, we imagined clashes of opponents parrying back and forth, one accusing the other of wasteful activity and the other insisting that the activity in question constituted a legitimate use. This was the case when critics accused TrackMeNot users of wasting bandwidth with searches that were of no genuine interest and TrackMeNot users responded that they weren't wasting bandwidth but rather were using it to promote legitimate privacy claims. Similarly, one who is accused of polluting a dataset or impairing a system's data-mining capacity counters that the purpose of the dataset or data mining is not one that warrants societal protection, or at least not one that should trump the obfuscator's evasion of surveillance.

Generally, asserting that data obfuscation impairs and damages a database or compromises a system, or that it overuses or wastes a common resource, doesn't entitle one to call the obfuscation unethical unless one can clearly explain how the data store or system in question furthers societal goals more important than contrary goals the obfuscator seeks to promote. Rarely are these conflicting ends explicitly or systematically addressed in ways that call on data collectors to justify the value of their activity. To understand the criterion of ends, you would ask about the purposes or values served by data collection—database or information flow—and the same for the obfuscating activities. Further, you would ask how these ends feature within broader political commitments of the collective—society, nation, etc. Thus far, we seem to give great leeway to the Transportation Security Administration's pursuit and assembly of personal information profiles insofar as its purposes are to provide security for travelers. Accordingly, we might be less tolerant of individuals who obfuscate in this context even for the purposes of protecting privacy, the point being that ends should make a difference in our reactions both to the ethics of data collection and to obfuscation.

But means matter, too. Even good ends may not justify all means. In law and policy, we are often asked to consider proportionality—for example, demanding that the punishment should fit the crime. Although an obfuscator must be challenged to justify means that are disruptive, even damaging, surely it is fair also to challenge the target. You may decide to install TrackMeNot not because you object to the basic practice of logging search queries but because you object to unacceptable extremes such as holding data with too much detail, for too long, without appropriate limits on use. Keeping data in order to improve search functions, even to match contextual ads to queries, may seem acceptable, but isn't it grossly disproportionate to a search engine's core function to hold data indefinitely in order to refine behavioral advertising and to match search histories with other online activity so as to profile people too personally, too precisely, too intimately? Such questions are relevant to all the extreme forms of information surveillance, with online surveillance a particular case in which ubiquitous tracking of online behavior seems wildly disproportionate as a means, insofar as it serves only the parochial ends of commercial advertising, even if this tracking slightly improves the efficacy of the ads. But the obfuscator, too, must answer the challenges of proportionality, and in quite concrete terms. Thus, we may agree that the ends of Track-MeNot are legitimate, but still want to regulate the volume of noise—say, to foil profiling but not to disable a search engine entirely with denial-of-service attacks. Drawing an exact line between proportional and disproportional is never easy, but the intuition that there is a line, even if it must be drawn case by case, is robust and deep.

Proportionality suggests normative standards for particular pairs of means and ends and pairs of actions and reactions, but means may also be measured by comparative standards, such as whether their cost is lower than that of alternatives. Utilitarian thinking is a case in point, demanding not only that the happiness yielded by actions or social policies under consideration should be greater than the unhappiness, or that the benefits should exceed the costs, but also that the actions or policies should yield the optimal proportion among available alternatives. Where obfuscation involves pulling the wool over someone's eyes, spoiling a dataset, or impairing the functioning of a system, even to achieve laudable ends, the ethical obfuscator still should investigate whether other means are as readily available with lesser moral costs. We can ask whether the costs associated with different forms of obfuscation vary significantly, but we also can ask whether other means might achieve the same goals without the costs we have been considering thus far.

The question of whether less disruptive but equally or more effective alternatives to obfuscation can be found is worth asking—although in chapter 3, where we reviewed some of the standard approaches to resisting troubling data-surveillance practices, we found little cause for optimism. Opting out, suggested by critics who say "If you don't like this practice, you can always choose not to engage," may be feasible when it comes to nifty mobile apps, digital games, and various forms of social media, but inconvenient and expensive when it comes to online shopping, EZ Pass, and Frequent Flyer programs—and forgoing many vectors of surveillance—mobile phones, credit cards, insurance, motor vehicles, public transportation—is now nearly infeasible for many people.

Other alternatives, including corporate best practices and legal regulation, though promising in theory, are limited in practice. For structural reasons having to do with radically misaligned interests and the proverbial folly of leaving the fox to guard the henhouse, meaningful limits on data practice aren't likely to be set by corporate actors. Further, a history of unsuccessful attempts to have various industries regulate their respective data practices leaves little hope for meaningful reform. Although governmental legislation has also been variably effective,[9] its effects haven't reached the commercial sector, particularly when it comes to regulating online and mobile tracking. Despite dogged efforts and the intense commitment of the Federal Trade Commission, the Department of Commerce's National Telecommunications and Information Administration, and other government agencies, general progress has been minimal. For example, notice and consent expressed in privacy policies remain the dominant mechanisms for protecting privacy online, despite decisive evidence that they are incomprehensible to data subjects, are expressed ambiguously, are continuously revised, and have not constrained the degree and scope of data collection and use in practice. Further, by most accounts, concerted efforts to establish a Do-Not-Track standard for Web browsing were sabotaged by the advertising industry,[10] and the Snowden revelations[11] have revealed that the U.S. government and other governments have long been conducting mass surveillance. Individuals have good reason to question whether their privacy interests in appropriate gathering and use of information will be secured any time soon by conventional means.

Justice and fairness

So far, we have shown that when obfuscators and their critics disagree over the ethics of obfuscation, their disagreements sometimes boil down to clashes over ends and values. The critic accuses the obfuscator of violating legitimate ends; the obfuscator accuses the target of precisely the same. Clashes such as these would benefit from public airing and deliberation in the political arena, something we strongly support. But in our discussion of ethics of obfuscation, we also identified clashes that concerned conflicting interests and preferences more than competing ends and values. A clear instance of this emerged in our discussion of free riding. Charged with unseemly behavior, obfuscators may point to the terms of interaction unilaterally set by data collectors, which enable the seizure by these data collectors of surplus value generated during the course of the interaction. In relation to peers, complaints of free riding have opened tricky questions, such as whether blame is more appropriately assigned to an obfuscator who may have exposed peers to even greater scrutiny or disadvantage or to the agents of that scrutiny or disadvantage.

A purely ethical resolution of such claims and counterclaims might not be possible when, taken in isolation, they amount to favoring either the obfuscator's interests and preferences or those of the obfuscator's target. Within a broader societal context, however, disputes over whose preferences and interests are given greatest credence are deeply political. They recognize certain entitlements over others, and in so doing they often bring about systematic allocation or reconfiguration of power, authority, and goods as well as of burdens and subjection. These are among the questions of justice and fairness that, for centuries, have troubled political philosophers when resolving clashes over what values trump other values and whose rights count more than the rights of others. Beyond rights and values, however, societies have sought principles to govern the distribution of a wide range of goods, to ameliorate deeply unfair, unjust, and indecent outcomes, rather than leaving it to brute competition among actors (individuals, institutions, and organizations), or to the fiat of incumbency as the strong incumbents would prefer.

To guide our reasoning about just and fair distribution of goods (power, wealth, authority, etc.), we have dipped into recent writings in political philosophy. We beg our readers' forbearance as we sample from a vast disciplinary tradition for insights that will help us address the standoff we have identified between target and obfuscator in all its particularities. It might seem unnecessary to drill down to first principles when technologically advanced, liberal, and progressive democracies would already presumably have integrated such principles into their laws and regulations. This would mean that we would need only to refer to existing law and regulation for answers to political questions concerning privacy and obfuscation. It is, however, precisely because existing laws and policies have not, or not yet, adequately confronted overwhelming gaps in privacy protection that the need exists to refer to fundamental principles for better answers.

Returning to situations in which obfuscators' resistance confounds a target's will or interests, we ask how these considerations of justice might guide our assessment. John Rawls, in *A Theory of Justice*,[12] demands as a basic requirement that the obfuscation practices in question not violate or erode basic rights and liberties. This requirement calls into question obfuscating systems relying on deception, system subversion, and exploitation that have the potential to violate rights of property, security, and autonomy. This principle establishes a presumption against such systems unless strong countervailing claims of equal or greater weight can clearly be demonstrated, including autonomy, fair treatment, freedom of speech, and freedom of political association—generally freedoms associated with a right to privacy. The first principle makes short work of obfuscation as used by criminals to mask their attacks and confuse their trails.

For nuanced cases in which neither adversary holds a clear ethical advantage in their competing claims, Rawls' second principle, that of *maximin*, is relevant. This principle demands that a just society should favor "the alternative the worst outcome of which is superior to the worst outcomes of the others."[13] In practical terms this means that when weighing policy options, a just society should not necessarily look to equalize the standing of different individuals or groups, but where this is not possible or makes no sense should focus on the plight of those on the lower end of the socioeconomic spectrum, ensuring that whatever policy is chosen is one that maximizes outcomes for these stakeholders. A just society's policies, in other words, should maximize the minimum.

Returning to earlier cases, let us now consider the debate over wasted resources—not common resources, which we have already addressed, but privately owned resources, as when obfuscation purportedly wastes Facebook's resources with misleading profiles. Here service providers and owners of resources declare that, because proprietary rights allow them to set terms of use at will and to their advantage, unauthorized actions, by definition, make unethical or wasteful use of their services or resources. Obfuscators, by contrast, claim that they are weakened, exploited, made vulnerable, and compromised, and that they are merely acting to rectify an imbalance of control, power, and advantage and to reduce risk and ambiguity. As was noted earlier, how we evaluate the competing claims affects whether we deem obfuscating activity, such as TrackMeNot's generating of fake queries, wasteful or legitimate, prohibited or allowed. Where no obvious ethical issue is at stake, these political choices about the exercise of power and privilege are subject to the maximin principle of justice. How this plays out will depend on details of specific instances—for example, concrete differences in the properties of TrackMeNot, Vula, and Russian nationalist Twitterbots, as well as the contexts in which they operate.

In relation to free riding, Rawls' second principle forces a question about whether the data services whose terms enable them to capture surplus value from personal information are entitled to that surplus value. It allows us to see that the entitlements of profit and control that these firms have unilaterally asserted through their terms of service are, in fact, open to redistribution through the adoption of different social policies. Obfuscators aren't free riding if the disadvantage of a particular engagement is excessive and unfair, and if the only claims they may be violating are those asserted by service providers under a regime that doesn't fully recognize its implications for information flows newly enabled by sociotechnical systems. A similar point applies to pollution. Although there are some who presume in favor of data collectors merely on the grounds that they have collected and assembled data and hence are entitled to its integrity, we believe that no charge of pollution will stick unless societal worth can be demonstrated. If that can't be done, an argument is needed to support the claim that any value should accrue only or mainly to the data collectors; it can't simply be presumed. Though it is true that individuals using obfuscation to take cover may diminish the purity of a data pool, impose costs on data gatherers, or deny data gatherers the benefits of surplus generated through collection, aggregation, and analysis of data, a full picture considers the value of the data and the legitimacy of data gatherers' claims. When there are charges of free riding or when there are charges of pollution, private claims of data owners and counterclaims of obfuscators are viewed as conflicts of preferences or interests. In our view, seeking resolution by pointing to property rights begs the question of the extent of these rights in the fluid environment of technology and data. This issue remains open to political negotiation and adjustment. General prosperity and societal welfare should be considered, ideally in light of Rawls' second principle.

Assignment of blame and moral responsibility may also be assessed politically. When considering liability for free riding and data pollution, we have argued that, although the obfuscator is a causal agent in both those cases, moral responsibility may nevertheless reasonably accrue to the target of obfuscation unless the target's activities and business or data practices are beyond reproach. Considerations of justice apply as much to fair distribution of costs as they do to fair distribution of benefits.[14]

In the various theories of justice offered by political philosophers, including Rawls, there is a fairly uniform idea of those on the bottom end of the socioeconomic spectrum toward whom great concern is directed. In highlighting various ways in which the maximin principle is relevant to the political standing of obfuscation, we have presumed traditional or standard views of what it means to be better off or worse off—powerful or weak, rich or poor, well or poorly educated, healthy or sick—remain relevant. To those dimensions of inequality, our theme of informational asymmetries of power and of knowledge adds two dimensions of difference between haves and have-nots, crucial to the maximin principle.[15]

Informational justice and the asymmetries of power and knowledge

Circumstances surrounding the obfuscating systems we introduced in part I of this book are typically characterized by both asymmetries of power and asymmetries of knowledge. The power differential between individuals and the corporate and governmental institutions and organizations that place them under surveillance, capture information about their activities, and subsequently assemble it and mine it is clear. The judging, preying eye of unspecified, digital publics[16] also may train its disciplining gaze on individuals. Although, as we demonstrated in part I, obfuscation can be and has been used by the more powerful against the less powerful, the more powerful usually have more direct ways to impose their will. Obfuscation is generally not as strong or certain as these more direct methods, and it is only rarely adopted by powerful actors—and then usually to evade the notice of other powerful actors.[17] Stronger actors have less of a need to resort to obfuscation because they have better methods available if they want to hide something—among them secret classifications, censorship, trade secrets, and threats of state violence. So let us consider the less powerful members of society who may reach for obfuscation to even the odds.

To people who are not well off or politically influential and not in a position to refuse terms of engagement, to people who aren't technically sophisticated or savvy enough to utilize strong encryption, and to people who want discounts at the supermarket, free email accounts, and cheap mobile phones, obfuscation offers some measure of resistance, obscurity, and dignity, if not a permanent reconfiguration of control or an inversion of the entrenched hierarchy. As Anatole France put it, "the law, in its majestic equality, forbids the rich as well as the poor to sleep under bridges and steal bread."[18] For those whom circumstance and necessity oblige to give up data about themselves—those who most need the shelter of the bridge, however ad hoc and unsatisfying it may be in comparison with a proper house—obfuscation provides a means of redress.

What we have called power asymmetries map closely onto traditional vectors of power—wealth, social class, education, race, and so forth. In today's data-driven societies, epistemic or information asymmetries are highly consequential. Obfuscation may provide cover against known, specific threats, but also may offer protection against lurking but poorly understood threats from uncertain sources (government or corporate), whose presence we sense but about which we know little. We suspect these "others" are able to capture information that we generate and emanate as we move about online, engage in transactions online and off, work, communicate, and socialize, but precisely what information they capture, where they send it, how it then is used, and the logic of its impact on us we simply do not know. This is the nature of the epistemic asymmetry in its most extreme form. Under these circumstances, obfuscation may seem like flailing about in the dark, but it offers some hope against the unknown knowers.

Obfuscating against direct exertions of power and control is resistance of a familiar kind, but the shield that obfuscation may promise against lurking, unknown adversaries calls to mind a different political threat. In his book *Republicanism: A Theory of Freedom and Government*, Philip Pettit prefers a definition of freedom not as actual non-interference but as non-domination—that is, security against arbitrary interference: "not just that people (or other actors, such as governments or corporations) with a power of arbitrary interference probably will not exercise it, but that the agents in question lose that power: they are deprived of the capacity to exercise it, or at least their capacity to exercise it is severely reduced."[19] Viewed from the weak side of the epistemic asymmetry, we may be aware that information about us and information emanating from our activities, online and off, is accessible to those higher up on the scale, often in the form of rationalized information assemblages—profiles that can be used to control us directly or indirectly and to decide what we can and can't have and where we can and can't go. As societies embrace the promise of big-data analytics, and as correlation and clustering assume a dominant role in decision making, individuals may increasingly be subjected to decisions that "work" statistically but don't "make sense."[20] Our freedom is compromised not only when we are prevented from having or doing what we want, but also when others have the capacity to exercise this power in ways that we don't understand and that we experience as arbitrary. Domination is precisely this, according to Pettit. Republicanism doesn't preclude non-arbitrary subjection to suitable forms of law and government; it requires only that individuals be secure against arbitrary interference, "controlled by the arbitrium—the will or judgment—of the interferer: to the extent, in particular, that it is not forced to track the interests and ideas of those who suffer the interference."[21]

Those on the wrong side of the power and knowledge asymmetries of an information society are, as we have argued, effectively class members of its less well-off —subjects of surveillance, uncertain how it affects their fates, and lacking power to set terms of engagement. Consequently, in developing policies for a society deemed just according to Rawls' two principles,[22] those on the wrong side of the asymmetries should be allowed the freedom to assert their values, interests, and preferences through obfuscation (in keeping with ethical requirements), even if this means impinging on the interests and preferences of those on the right side of knowledge and power asymmetries. Thus, having seen to the ethics requirements of the first principle, according to the second, maximin principle, social policy aimed at resolving conflicting interests and preferences inherent in cases we have discussed should take heed of the important work these are doing potentially to raise the standing of those on the losing end of entrenched power and knowledge asymmetries.

For the welfare of others

We end this section with what may well be the toughest challenge confronting data obfuscation: whether it can be tolerated when it aims at systems that promise societal benefits extending beyond the individual subjects themselves. As we enter deeper and deeper into the epistemic and decision-making paradigm of big data, and as hope is stoked by its potential to serve the common good, questions arise concerning the obligation of individuals to participate.[23] Obfuscators may be faulted for being unwilling to pay costs for benefits, failing to pitch in for the sake of the common good. But what exactly is the extent of this obligation, and its limits? Are individuals obligated to pay whatever is asked, succumb to any terms of service, and pitch in even if there is a cost? Do sufferers from a rare disease, for example, owe it to others to participate in studies, and to allow data about them to be integrated into statistical analyses in which the size of N improves the results? And what if there is a cost?

The plight of the ethical obfuscator resembles that of the ethical citizen expected to contribute to the common good by, say, paying taxes or serving in the military. Some might say, equivalently, that we must fulfill an obligation not only by contributing to the common store of data but also by doing so honestly, accurately, and conscientiously. Even if there is some sense of obligation, what principles govern its shape, particularly if there is risk or cost associated with it? Ethics, generally, doesn't require supererogation, and liberal democracies don't demand or condone the sacrifice of innocent individuals, even a few, for the benefit of the majority. Where to draw the line? What principles of justice offer guidance on these matters?

Jeremy Waldron observed that after the terrorist attacks of September 11, 2001 citizens were asked to allow the balance of security and liberty to be tipped in favor of security.[24] Although it isn't unusual for social policy to require tradeoffs—one value, one right against another or others—Waldron reminds us that such tradeoffs must be made wisely with fastidious attention to consequences. One particular consequence is the distributional impact; losses and gains, costs and benefits should be borne fairly among individuals and between groups. Waldron's worry is that when we say that *we* collectively give up a measure of freedom in return for *our* collective security there is an important elision: some individuals or groups suffer a disproportionate loss of freedom for the security benefit of all, or, as sometimes happens with tradeoffs in general, may even be excluded entirely from the collective benefits. Generalizing this warning to questions about paying for the collective good with individual data prompts us to consider not only the total sum of costs over benefits but also who is paying the cost and who is enjoying the benefits. Often, companies defend data avarice by citing service improvements or security but are vague about crucial details—for example, whether existing customers and data contributors are supporting new ones who haven't pitched in, and what proportion of the value extracted accrues to "all" and what proportion to the company. These questions must be answered in order to address questions about the nature and extent of the obligations data subjects have to contribute to the common data store.

Risk and data

The language of risk frequently crops up in hailing the promise of big data for the good of all. Proponents would have us believe that data will help reduce risks of terror and crime, of inefficacious medical treatment, of bad credit decisions, of inadequate education, of inefficient energy use, and so forth. These claims should persuade or even compel individuals to give generously of information, as we graciously expose the contents of our suitcases in airports. By the logic of these claims, obfuscators are unethical in diminishing, depriving, or subverting the common stock. Persuasive? Irrefutable? Yet here, too, justice demands attention to distribution and fairness: who risks and who benefits? We do not flatly reject the claims, but until these questions are answered and issues of harm and costs are addressed there can be no such obligation. Take, for example, the trivial and ubiquitous practice of online tracking for the purpose of behavioral advertising.[25] Ad networks claim that online tracking and behavioral advertising reduce the "risk" of costly advertising to unsuitable targets or to targeting attractive offers to unprofitable customers. Risk reduction it may indeed be, but information contributions by all are improving the lot only of a few, primarily the ad networks providing the service, possibly the advertisers, and perhaps the attractive customers they seek to lure. We made a similar point above when we discussed data aggregation for the purpose of reducing credit fraud: that citing risk reduction often oversimplifies a picture in which risk may not be reduced overall, or even if it is reduced, not reduced *for* all. What actually occurs is that risk is shifted and redistributed. We offer similar cautions against inappropriate disclosure of medical information, which may increase risk for some information subjects while decreasing it for others; or collecting and mining data for the purposes of price discrimination, imposing risks on consumers under surveillance while reducing risks for merchants who engage in schemes of data profiling.

In sum

Data obfuscation raises important ethical challenges that anyone designing or using obfuscating systems would do well to heed. We have scrutinized the challenges and explored contexts and conditions that are relevant to their adjudication in ethical terms. But we also have discovered that adjudicating ethical challenges often invokes considerations that are political and expedient. Politics comes into play when disputes hinge on disagreements over the relative importance of societal ends and relative significance of ethical and societal values. It also comes into play when addressing the merits of competing non-moral claims, the allocation of goods, and the distribution of risks. When entering the realms of the political, obfuscation must be tested against the demands of justice. But if obfuscators are so tested, so must we test the data collectors, the information services, the trackers, and the profilers. We have found that breathless rhetoric surrounding the promise and practice of data does not say enough about justice and the problem of risk shifting. Incumbents have embedded few protections and mitigations into the edifices of data they are constructing. Against this backdrop, obfuscation offers a means of striving for balance defensible when it functions to resist domination of the weaker by the stronger. A just society leaves this escape hatch open.

5 WILL OBFUSCATION WORK?

How can obfuscation succeed? How can the efforts of a few individuals generating extraneous data work against well-funded, determined institutions, let alone against such behemoths of data as Google, Facebook, Axciom, and the National Security Agency? Encountering these doubts again and again, we have come to see that when people ask about particular instantiations of obfuscation, or obfuscation generally "But does it *work?*" the reasonable answer is "Yes, but it depends." It depends on the goals, the obfuscator, the adversary, the resources available, and more. These, in turn, suggest means, methods, and principles for design and execution.

The typical scenario we imagined earlier involves individuals functioning within information ecosystems often not of their own making or choosing. Against the designers, operators, managers, and owners of these ecosystems, individual data subjects stand in an asymmetric relation of knowledge, power, or both. Although these individuals are aware that information about them or produced by them is necessary for the relationship, there is much that they don't know. How much is taken? What is done with it? How will they be affected? They may grasp enough about the ecosystems in which they are wittingly or unwittingly enrolled, from Web searching to facial recognition, to believe or recognize that its practices are inappropriate, but, at the same time, recognize that they aren't capable of reasonably functioning outside it, or of reasonably inducing change within it.

Whether obfuscation works—whether unilateral shifting of terms of engagement over personal information is fulfilled by a particular obfuscation project—may seem to be a straightforward question about a specific problem-solving technique, but upon closer scrutiny it is actually several questions. Whether obfuscation works depends on characteristics of the existing circumstances, the desired alteration in terms, what counts as fulfillment of these desires, and the architecture and features of the particular obfuscation project under consideration. This is why answering the question "Does it work?" with "It depends" isn't facetious; instead it is an invitation to consider in systematic terms what characteristics of an information ecosystem make it one in which obfuscation could work. Beyond these considerations, we seek to map design possibilities for obfuscation projects into an array of diverse goals that the instigators and users of such projects may have.

Therefore, we have to answer two questions with this chapter. We can take the question "Will obfuscation work?" in the sense "How can obfuscation work for me and my particular situation?" or in the sense "Does obfuscation work in general?" We will respond to both questions. The overall answer is straightforward: Yes, obfuscation can work, but whether it does and to what extent depends on how it is implemented to respond to a threat, fulfill a goal, and meet other specific parameters. This chapter presents a set of questions that we think should be addressed if obfuscation is to be applied well.

5.1 Obfuscation is about goals

In the world of security and privacy theory, it is by now well established that the answer to every "Does it work?" question is "It depends." To secure something, to make it private or safe or secret, entails tradeoffs, many of which we have already discussed. Securing things requires time, money, effort, and attention, and adds organizational and personal friction while diminishing convenience and access to many tools and services. Near-total freedom from digital surveillance for an individual is simple, after all: just lead the life of an undocumented migrant laborer of the 1920s, with no Internet, no phones, no insurance, no assets, riding the rails, being paid off the books for illegal manual work. Simple, but with a very high cost, because the threat model of "everything" is ludicrously broad. When we think of organizational security tradeoffs, we can think of the "Cone of Silence" in the spy-movie-parody television series *Get Smart*.[1] Used for conducting top secret meetings, the Cone works so well that the people in it can't hear one another—it is perfectly private and amusingly useless.[2]

Threat models lower the costs of security and privacy by helping us understand what our adversaries are looking for and what they are capable of finding, so that we can defend against those dangers specifically.[3] If you know that your organization faces a danger that includes sophisticated attacks on its information security, you should fill in all the USB ports on the organization's computers with rubber cement and keep sensitive information on "airgapped" machines that are never connected to the network. But if you don't believe that your organization faces such a danger, why deprive people of the utility of USB sticks? Obfuscation in general is useful in relation to a specific type of threat, shaped by *necessary visibility*. As we have emphasized throughout, the obfuscator is already exposed to some degree—visible to radar, to people scrutinizing public legal filings, to security cameras, to eavesdropping, to Web search providers, and generally to data collection defined by the terms of service. Furthermore, he or she is exposed, to a largely unknown degree, at the wrong side of the information asymmetry, and this unknown exposure is further aggravated by time—by future circulation of data and systems of analysis. We take this visibility as a starting point for working out the role that obfuscation can play.

To put that another way, we don't have a best-practices threat model available—in fact, an obfuscator may not have sufficient resources, research, or training to put such a model together. We are operating from a position of weakness, obligated to accept choices we should probably refuse. If this is the case, we have to make do (more on that below) and we must have a clear sense of what we want to accomplish. Consider danah boyd's research on American teenagers' use of social media. Teens in the United States are subject to an enormous amount of scrutiny, almost all of it without their consent or control (parents, school, other authority figures). Social media would seem to make them subject to even more. They are exposed to scrutiny by default—in fact, it is to their benefit, from a privacy perspective, to appear to be visible to everyone. "As teens encounter particular technologies, they make decisions based on what they're trying to achieve," boyd writes,[4] and what they are trying to achieve is often to share content without sharing *meaning*. They can't necessarily create secret social spaces for their community—parents can and do demand passwords to their social-network accounts and access to their phones. Instead, they use a variety of practices that assume everyone can see what they do, and then behave so that only a few people can understand the meaning of their actions. "Limiting access to meaning," boyd writes, "can be a much more powerful tool for achieving privacy than trying to limit access to the content itself."[5] Their methods don't necessarily use obfuscation (they lean heavily on subtle social cues, references, and nuance to create material that reads differently to different audiences, a practice of "social steganography"), but they emphasize the importance of understanding goals. The goal is not to disappear or to maintain total informational control (which may be impossible); it is to limit and shape the community that can accurately interpret actions that everyone can see.

Much the same is true of obfuscation. Many instances and practices that we have gathered under that heading are expressions of particular goals that take discovery, visibility, or vulnerability as a starting point. For all the reasons we have already discussed, people now can't escape certain kinds of data collection and analysis, so the question then becomes "What does the obfuscator want to do with obfuscation?" The answer to that question gives us a set of parameters (choices, constraints, mechanisms) that we can use to shape our approach to obfuscation.

5.2 I want to use obfuscation ...

A safe that can't be cracked does not exist. Safes are rated in hours—in how long it would take an attacker (given various sets of tools) to open them.[6] A safe is purchased as a source of security in addition to other elements of security, including locked doors, alarms, guards, and law-enforcement personnel. A one-hour safe with an alarm probably is adequate in a precinct where the police reliably show up in twenty minutes. If we abstract this a little bit, we can use it to characterize the goals of obfuscation. The strength of an obfuscation approach isn't measured by a single objective standard (as safes are) but in relation to a goal and a context: to be *strong enough*. It may be used on its own or in concert with other privacy techniques. The success of obfuscation is always relative to its purposes, and to consideration of constraints, obstacles, and the un-level playing field of epistemic and power asymmetries.

When gathering different obfuscation examples, we observed that there was convergence around general aims and purposes that cropped up numerous times, even though a single system could be associated with several ends or purposes and even though intermediate ends sometimes served as means to achieve other ends. There are subtler distinctions, too, but we have simplified and unified purposes and ends into goals to make them more readily applicable to design and practice. They are arranged roughly in order of inclusion, from buying time to expressing protest. Interfering with profiling, the fifth goal, can include some of the earlier goals, such as providing cover, within it, and can be in turn contained by expressing protest (the sixth goal). (Since virtually all obfuscation contributes to the difficulty of rapidly analyzing and processing data for surveillance purposes, all the higher-order goals include the first goal: buying time.) As you identify the goal suited to your project, you ascend a ladder of complexity and diversity of possible types of obfuscation.

Skeptical readers—and we all should be skeptical—will notice that we are no longer relying heavily on examples of obfuscation used by powerful groups for malign ends, such as the use of Twitter bots to hamper election protests, the use of likefarming in social-network scams, or inter-business corporate warfare. We want this section to focus on how obfuscation can be used for positive purposes.

If you can answer the questions in the previous chapter to your satisfaction, then this chapter is intended for you. We begin with the possibility that you want to use obfuscation to buy some time.

... to buy some time

Did radar chaff "work"? After all, it fluttered to the ground in minutes, leaving the sky again open for the sweep of the beam—but of course by then the plane was already out of range.

The ephemeral obfuscation systems meant to *buy time* are, in a sense, elegantly simple, but they require a deep appreciation of intricate physical, scientific, technical, social, and cultural surroundings. Success doesn't require that one buy a particular amount of time, or the longest time possible; it requires only that one buy just enough time. Using identical confederates, or even just slowing the process of going through documents, dealing with bureaucracy, or sorting true from false information, can work toward this end. Most obfuscation strategies work best in concert with other techniques of privacy protection or protest, but this is particularly true of time-buying approaches, which rely on other means of evasion and resistance already being in place—and a very clear sense of the adversary. (See the questions in section 5.3.)

... to provide cover

This subsection and the next are related but distinct, with a substantial overlap. They approach the same problem from different sides: keeping an adversary from definitively connecting particular activities, outcomes, or objects to an actor. Obfuscation for cover involves concealing the action in the space of other actions. Some approaches can be implemented to withstand scrutiny; others rely on the cover provided by context to escape observation. Think of babble tapes, which bury a message in dozens of channels of voices: we know that the speaker is speaking, but we don't know what is being said. Or think of the approach that Operation Vula ultimately settled on: not simply encrypted email, but encrypted email that would perfectly fit the profile of banal international business. The communications of ANC operatives could take on cover as an additional layer of protection (along with crypto and superb operational security) by using the traffic of other messages similar to theirs to avoid observation. One method assumes scrutiny, and the other strives to be ignored; each is suited to its situation.

... for deniability

If providing cover hides the action in the space of other actions, providing deniability hides the *decision*, making it more difficult to connect an action and an actor with certainty. One of the benefits of running a Tor relay is the additional layer of confusion it creates: is this traffic starting with you, or are you just passing it along for someone else? (TrackMeNot has a similar mechanism; we will discuss it in greater detail in the subsection on interference with profiling.) Likewise, consider the use of simulated uploads to leak sites, which make it harder to determine definitively that a certain file was uploaded during a session by some particular IP address. Finally, think of something as simple as shuffling SIM cards around: it doesn't conceal the activity of carrying phones and placing calls, but makes it more difficult to be certain that it's *this* person with *this* phone at any time. Though providing deniability blurs a bit with providing cover and with preventing individual observation, it is particularly useful when you know that your adversary wants to be sure that it has the right person.

... to prevent individual exposure

This somewhat unusual goal may at first sound generic (don't all obfuscation approaches want to prevent individual observation?), but we mean something very specific by it. Certain obfuscation approaches are well suited to achieving the positive social outcome of enabling individuals, companies, institutions, and governments to use aggregate data while keeping the data from being used to observe any *particular* person. Privacy-preserving participatory sensing can collect valuable aggregate data about traffic flows without revealing anything reliable about one particular vehicle. CacheCloak retains the significant social utility of location-based mobile services while preventing the providers of those services from tracking the users (and leaving open other avenues to making money). Pools for the swapping of loyalty cards give grocery and retail chains most of the benefits they were hoping for (the cards are driving business their way and providing useful demographic data, postal codes, or data on purchases) but prevent them from compiling dossiers on specific shoppers.

... to interfere with profiling

Another rung up the ladder of comprehensiveness, anti-profiling obfuscation may interfere with observation of individuals or with analysis of a group, may provide cover or deniability, or may raise the cost (in time and money) of the business of data. It may leave aggregate useful data intact or may pack it with ambiguity, reasonable lies, and nonsense.

Vortex was a cookie-swapping system that enabled users to hop between identities and profiles. Had it been widely implemented beyond the prototype stage, it would have rendered online profiling for advertising purposes useless. The various "cloning" and disinformation services we have described offer similar tools for making profiling less reliable. TrackMeNot provides search-query deniability (e.g., was that query about "Tea Party join" or "fluffy sex toys" from you, or not?) under the larger goal of rendering search profiles in general less reliable. Which queries can you trust? Which queries define the cluster into which the searcher fits? Against which queries should you serve ads, and what user activity and identities should you provide in response to a subpoena?

... to express protest

Of course, TrackMeNot is a gesture of protest, as are many of our other examples—for example, card-swapping activists and crowds in Guy Fawkes masks. Many obfuscation strategies can meet or contribute to goals already mentioned while also serving to register discontent or refusal. A pertinent question to ask of your obfuscation approach is whether it is intended to keep you unnoticed, to make you seem innocuous, or to make your dissent known.

5.3 Is my obfuscation project ...

Now that you have a sense of your goals, we can turn to four remaining questions that build on the goals and shape the components of an obfuscation project. As was true of the six goals, there is some overlap between these questions. They will determine how an obfuscation system works, but they are not perfectly distinct, and they have some effect on each other. We have separated them according to the roles they play in implementing obfuscation.

... individual, or collective?

Can your obfuscation project be carried out effectively by one person, or does it require collective action? One person wearing a mask is *more* easily identified and tracked than someone not wearing a mask, but a hundred people wearing the same mask become a crowd of collective identity, and that makes individual attribution of actions difficult. Some obfuscation projects can be used by an individual or by a small group but will become more effective as more people join in. The reverse could also be true (see "known or unknown," below): a technique that relies on blending in and not being noticed—that functions by avoiding scrutiny—will become far more vulnerable if widely adopted.

Two consequences will follow from your answer to the question this sub-section asks.

First, an obfuscation technique that builds on collective action can spur adoption through the "network effect." If the technique becomes more reliable or more robust for all existing users as more users join, you can think about the design from the perspective of crossing that threshold where significant gains for joining become apparent and you can spark widespread use. Does your technique require some number of users before it will be really effective? If it does, how will you get it to that point? This is an opportunity to think about whether the technique can "scale"—whether it can continue to provide utility once it is being rapidly taken up in large numbers. This also bears on usability: a technique that requires a number of users to succeed should have a lot of thought put into how immediately useable, understandable, and friendly it is. If your obfuscation requires a number of users, then the plan must include how to get them. The Tor project, for example, has recognized the need for greater accessibility to non-expert users.

Second, a technique that relies on relative obscurity—on not being widely adopted, or on not being something that an adversary is looking for—benefits from exclusivity.

... known, or unknown?

Some obfuscation methods use their ability to blend into the innocuous data they generate to avoid scrutiny; others use it to *escape* scrutiny. For the goals you want to accomplish, can your method work if your adversary knows it is being employed, or if your adversary is familiar in detail with how it works?

For many techniques that merely buy time, the answer doesn't matter. For example, whether or not the adversary's radar operator thinks a large number of dots represent real airplanes makes no difference to the adversary's ability to coordinate a counterattack. As long as the radar operator is slowed down for ten minutes, the obfuscation provided by chaff is a success. More complex obfuscation methods can accomplish different goals depending on whether or not the adversary knows they are being used. For example, if AdNauseam activity isn't known to the adversary, it works to foil profiling, filling the record of advertising clicks with indiscriminate, meaningless activity. If it is known, it both frustrates the work of profiling the individual and develops a protest role—a known gesture of mocking refusal. (Build a surveillance machine to get me to click a few ads? I'll click all of them!)

However, in some cases the distinction matters and must be accounted for. If your goal is to render a database less effective or less valuable in the long term, so that your adversary continues to use it and thus is acting on misleading or false information, you want sources of plausible obfuscation to remain unknown so they can't be selected and expunged or countered. Forms of obfuscation that function primarily as acts of public protest need their obfuscating nature to be made explicit so they can stand as refusal rather than compliance.

... selective, or general?

This is the most complex of the questions, with four different implications that must be considered.

Each of the goals discussed above, to one degree or another, relies on an understanding of the adversary against which obfuscation is directed. Often this understanding—whether it is formalized as a threat model or whether it is informed guesswork—is fragmentary, missing important components, or otherwise compromised. What first interested us in obfuscation was its use by people who often lacked precise mastery of the challenge they faced to their privacy: it was proprietary, or classified, or it relied on technologies and techniques they could not comprehend, or the "adversaries" included other people freely giving up their data, or the problem existed both in the present and in possible future vulnerabilities. In addition to having a clear understanding of the limits of obfuscation—that, knowing one's adversary—we must bear in mind what we don't know, and beware of relying on any one technique alone to protect sensitive information. This raises the question of how *directed* a particular obfuscation strategy is. Is it a general attempt at covering one's tracks, or is the obfuscating noise that you produce tailored to a particular threat about which you have some knowledge? A few further questions follow from your answer to this.

First, is your obfuscation approach directed at a specific adversary, or is it directed at *anyone* who might be gathering and making use of data about you? Is there a specific point of analysis you are delaying or preventing, or are you just trying to kick up as much dust as you can? The strategy outlined in the "cloning" patent that Apple acquired is an example of the latter: producing many variants of the user, all generating plausible data, for anyone who might be collecting. If you know your adversary and know your adversary's techniques and goals, you can be much more precise in your obfuscation.

If you know your adversary, a second question arises: Is that adversary targeting you (or a select group), or are you subject to a more general aggregation and analysis of data? If the former, you must find ways to selectively misrepresent your data. The latter possibility offers a different task for the obfuscator: the production of misleading data can take a significantly wider-ranging form, resembling data on what may be many individuals.

This, in turn, raises a third question: Is your technique supposed to provide selective benefit, or general benefit? In view of how much of the work of data surveillance is not about scrutinizing individuals but rather is about using inferences derived from larger groups, your method might work to obfuscate only your own tracks, or it might work to render overall profiles and models less reliable. Each of those possibilities presents its own distinct difficulties. For example, if TrackMeNot functions effectively, it has the capacity to cast doubt not only on the obfuscator's profile but also on the profiles of others in the dataset.

Thinking about beneficiaries raises a fourth question: Is your goal to produce data of general illegibility, so no one knows or needs to know what is real and what is obfuscation? Or is it to produce obfuscated data that an adversary can't get any value from (or can get only diminished value from), but that tell the truth to those who need to know what is real? Think of FaceCloak, a system that keeps Facebook from gaining access to personal data by providing it with meaningless noise while keeping the actual, salient personal and social data available to one's friends. Or consider a system designed to preserve socially valuable classes of data – derived from the census, for example, in order to allocate resources effectively or to govern efficiently, while preventing the identification of individual data subjects within them. Creating a selectively readable system is far more challenging than simply making generally plausible lies, but a selectively readable system offers wider benefits along with privacy protection, and the difficulties involved in creating it are a challenge that should be accounted for at the outset of a project.

... short-term, or long-term?

Finally, over how long a time span should your project be effective? The goal of buying time is a starting place for answering this question. If you want to confuse the situation for only ten minutes, that's one thing; if you want to render some database *permanently* unreliable, untrustworthy, and valueless for inference or prediction, that's much harder. A major component of the information asymmetry that obfuscation helps to address is temporal—the "time-traveling robots from the future" problem we discussed in chapter 3. Certain data may be innocuous now, but a change in context, a change in ownership, or tools or laws can make the same data dangerous. Does your technique have to work only for now, and only for one outrage, one company, and one technique of collection and analysis, or does it have to ruin the data so that they can't be trusted in the future or for other purposes? The former isn't easy but is relatively straightforward. The latter involves a much broader set of challenges. It is worthwhile to consider this question now, at the development stage, so as not to be caught out after a technique has been widely adopted and you realize that it was provisional, or that it was particular to a company bound by certain national laws that no longer apply.

With these six goals and four questions in mind, we can assess the fundamentals—and some of the pitfalls—of putting together an obfuscation strategy. Of course, the questions won't end with these. As viable practice, as a powerful and credible response to oppressive data regimes, obfuscation will be well served by conditions that will enable it to develop and thrive. These include the following:

• *Progress in relevant sciences and engineering* Develop methods in statistics, cryptography, systems engineering, machine learning, system security, networking, and threat modeling that address questions like: how much noise, what kind of noise, how to tailor for the target of noise, how to protect against attack, and for what specific problems is obfuscation the right solution?

• *Progress in relevant social sciences, theory, and ethics* Address questions about what individuals want and need in their uses of obfuscating systems, and to engage in sound normative assessments of proposed systems.

• *Progress in technology policy and regulation* Safeguard open and public standards and protocols that allow developers of obfuscating systems access to and engagement with critical infrastructure; encourage large, public facing systems to offer open APIs to developers of obfuscating systems; and refuse enforcement of Terms of Service that prohibit reasonable obfuscating systems.

Obfuscation, in its humble, provisional, better-than-nothing, socially contingent way, is deeply entangled with the context of use. Are you creating a personal act of refusal, designed to stand on its own as a gesture of protest, whether or not it actually makes data collection less useful? Are you using obfuscation as one element in a larger suite of privacy-protection tools tailored to a group and an adversary—obfuscation that has to work verifiably in relation to a specific data-analysis strategy? Perhaps you are applying obfuscation at the level of policy, or to data collection that requires more effort to misuse, so as to increase the cost of indiscriminate surveillance. Or perhaps you are developing or contributing to software that can provide a service with a layer of obfuscation that makes it difficult to do anything *but* provide the service. You may have access to considerable technical, social, political, and financial resources, or you may be filling out forms, dealing with institutions, or interacting online without much choice in the matter. With all of those different possibilities, however, the issues raised by our goals and questions are general to obfuscation projects across different domains, and working through them provides a starting point for getting your obfuscation work out into the world, where it can begin doing good by making noise.

EPILOGUE

We didn't invent obfuscation. We started out with a tool for the specific purpose of interfering with search-query logs, then recognized that it did something we could see all around us. We undertook the task of naming it and clarifying its most important parts so it could be generalized, and so it could serve as the beginnings of a method that can play a role in addressing some of the most intractable privacy challenges of information technologies, communications networks, and data collection and analysis. Once we started looking, we were amazed by the range of applications we uncovered. In part I of this book, we offered a compendium of the possibilities.

In part II, we laid out the concept of data obfuscation as a strategy for privacy protection, the ethical issues obfuscation raises, and some salient questions to ask of any obfuscation project. Throughout, we took care to emphasize that obfuscation is an addition to the privacy toolkit, not a replacement for one or all of the tools on which we already rely. It has a role to play as part of a rich network of tools, theories, frameworks, skills, and equipment that enable us to respond to present-day threats to privacy. We have only begun the work by naming, identifying, and defining. This book is a collection of starting points for understanding and making use of obfuscation. There is much more to be learned from practice, from *doing*.

We have described cases of obfuscation working in concert with other approaches to privacy protection and how obfuscation may be integrated with law, social media, policy and encryption to augment the effectiveness of these alternatives. Given the range of obfuscation goals, from buying time to foiling profiling to protesting, can we develop different models of success with quantifiable metrics? Of course, obfuscation is shaped by its relationship to an adversary, but most of the situations in which it is used involve various kinds and degrees of uncertainty—uncertainty about what can be done with data, about how these capabilities expand when data sets are combined, and the other mysteries inherent in the information asymmetries that characterize everyday life. For obfuscation projects specifically seeking to provide deniability or cover, or to interfere with profiling (especially over the longer term), can we develop optimal obfuscation methods under different kinds of uncertainty? Can we take sophisticated present-day methods of data analysis, such as advanced neural networks and deep learning, and use them to develop more effective obfuscation strategies? We have identified common goals and have uncovered crucial questions, but are there best practices for putting obfuscation into play that apply across different obfuscation projects? These are questions to be answered with further research and application. Others will follow as the utility of obfuscation makes evident its promise, at least until such time as the need for firmer and fairer approaches to regulating appropriate data practices is properly addressed.

There is no simple solution to the problem of privacy, because privacy itself is a solution to societal challenges that are in constant flux. Some are natural and beyond our control; others are technological and should be within our control but are shaped by a panoply of complex social and material forces with indeterminate effects. Privacy does not mean stopping the flow of data; it means channeling it wisely and justly to serve societal ends and values and the individuals who are its subjects, particularly the vulnerable and the disadvantaged. Privacy should sustain the freedoms and autonomous pursuits that fuel positive engagement with one another and with the collective. Innumerable customs, concepts, tools, laws, mechanisms, and protocols have evolved to achieve privacy, so conceived, and it is to that collection that we add obfuscation to sustain privacy as an active conversation, a struggle, and a choice.

Having considered obfuscation through cases, instances, explanations, and ethical questions, and having considered its effectiveness and its fitness for various purposes, you may want to set the book aside and consider implementing obfuscation, in software or in policy, for a project you run or a project you resist—to create a crowd and vanish into it, for your benefit, the benefit of others, and the benefit of learning by doing.

NOTES

CHAPTER 1

1. Meir Finkel, *On Flexibility: Recovery from Technological and Doctrinal Surprise on the Battlefield* (Stanford University Press, 2011), 125.

2. Fred Cohen, "The Use of Deception Techniques: Honeypots and Decoys," in *Handbook of Information Security*, volume 3, ed. Hossein Bidgoli (Wiley, 2006), 646.

3. Kirill Maslinsky, Sergey Koltcov, and Olessia Koltslova, "Changes in the Topical Structure of Russian-Language LiveJournal: The Impact of Elections 2011," Research Paper WP BPR 14/SOC/2013, National Research University, Moscow, 3. For recent data on the proportion of LiveJournal users by country, see http://www.alexa.com/siteinfo/livejournal.com.

4. The LiveJournal statistics cited here are from http://www.livejournal.com/stats.bml. (This site is no longer available.)

5. Simon Shuster, "Why Have Hackers Hit Russia's Most Popular Blogging Service?" time.com, April 7, 2011 (http://content.time.com/time/world/article/0,8599,2063952,00.html). (The number of Russian accounts cited in the article appears to be the total number of accounts rather than the number of active accounts. We believe activity to be a more meaningful measure.)

6. Yekaterina Parkhomenko and Arch Tait, "Blog Talk," *Index on Censorship* 37 (February 2008): 174–178 (doi:10.1080/03064220701882822).

7. Suren Gazaryan, "Russia: Control From the Top Down," Enemies of the Internet, March 11, 2014 (http://12mars.rsf.org/2014-en/2014/03/11/russia-repression-from-the-top-down/).

8. Brian Krebs, "Twitter Bots Drown Out Anti-Kremlin Tweets," Krebs on Security, December 11, 2008 (http://krebsonsecurity.com/2011/12/twitter-bots-drown-out-anti-kremlin-tweets/).

9. Ann Friedman, "Hashtag Journalism," *Columbia Journalism Review* #realtalk blog, May 29, 2014 (http://www.cjr.org/realtalk/hashtag_journalism.php?page=all).

10. "Twitterbots," Krebs on Security (http://krebsonsecurity.com/wp-content/uploads/2011/12/twitterbots1.txt).

11. Manuel Reda, "Mexico: Twitterbots Sabotage Anti-PRI Protest," Fusion, May 21, 2012 (http://thisisfusion.tumblr.com/post/23287767289/twitterbots-attack-anti-pri -protest-mexico).

12. For a more direct application of Twitter spam in the Mexican election that skirts this rule, see Mike Orcutt, "Twitter Mischief Plagues Mexico's Election," *MIT Technology Review*, June 21, 2014 (http://www.technologyreview.com/news/428286/twitter -mischief-plagues-mexicos-election/).

13. Joseph Meyerowitz and Romit R. Choudhury, "Hiding Stars with Fireworks: Location Privacy through Camouflage," in *Proceedings of the 15th Annual International Conference on Mobile Computing and Networking* (ACM, 2009).

14. Ibid., 1.

15. Daniel Howe and Helen Nissenbaum, "TrackMeNot: Resisting Surveillance in Web Search," in *Lessons From the Identity Trail: Anonymity, Privacy and Identity in a Networked Society*, ed. Ian Kerr, Carole Luckock, and Valerie Steeves (Oxford University Press, 2009), 417.

16. For the AOL search logs event, see Michael Barbaro and Tom Zeller Jr., "A Face Is Exposed for AOL Searcher No. 4417749," *New York Times*, August 9, 2006. For the Department of Justice's Google request, see the original subpoena: *Gonzales v. Google, Inc.*, Case (Subpoena) CV 06-8006MISC JW (N.D. Cal.). http://www.google.com/press/images/subpoena_20060317.pdf, and the consequent ruling: *American Civil Liberties Union v. Gonzalez*, Case 98-5591 (E.D. Pa.) (http://www.google.com/press/images/ruling_20060317.pdf).

17. Note, for instance, that the rollout information for Google's more personalized search results—building on Google+ information—includes a toggle that enables you to see your results without the effect of your history of searching the Web. This doesn't remove the history, but it presents query history as something that should at least be optional, and not as an unalloyed good. See Amit Singhal, "Search, Plus Your World," Google official blog (http://googleblog.blogspot.com/2012/01/search-plus -your-world.html), January 10, 2012.

18. Vincent Toubiana and Helen Nissenbaum, "An Analysis of Google Logs Retention Policies," *Journal of Privacy and Confidentiality* 3, no. 1 (2011): 3–26 (http://repository. cmu.edu/jpc/vol3/iss1/2/).

19. Andy Greenberg, *This Machine Kills Secrets: How WikiLeakers, Cypherpunks, and Hacktivists Aim to Free the World's Information* (Dutton, 2012), 157.

20. Ibid., 293.

21. Phil Hellmuth, Marvin Karlins, and Joe Navarro, *Phil Hellmuth Presents Read 'Em and Reap* (HarperCollins, 2006). (It is interesting to imagine a poker strategy based on more extensive use of obfuscation—a player generating a constant stream of mannerisms and typical tells, so that anything involuntary is difficult to parse out—but that probably would be so irritating as to get a player ejected.)

22. Wesley Remmer, "Learning the Secret Language of Baseball," *Bremerton Patriot*, July 23, 2010 (http://www.bremertonpatriot.com/sports/99124354.html).

23. *Spartacus*, directed by Stanley Kubrick (Universal Pictures, 1960).

24. Charles Dickens, *A Tale of Two Cities* (Penguin Classics, 2003); Alan Moore and David Lloyd, *V for Vendetta* (Vertigo/DC Comics, 1982).

25. Marco Deseriis, "Lots of Money Because I Am Many: The Luther Blissett Project and the Multiple-Use Name Strategy," *Thamyris/Intersecting* 21 (2011): 65–93.

26. *The Thomas Crown Affair*, directed by John McTiernan (Metro-Goldwyn-Mayer, 1999).

27. *Inside Man*, directed by Spike Lee (Universal Pictures, 2006).

28. *North by Northwest*, directed by Alfred Hitchcock (Metro-Goldwyn-Mayer, 1959).

29. Thomas Habinek, *The World of Roman Song: From Ritualized Speech to Social Order* (Johns Hopkins University Press, 2005), 10.

30. Arthur Conan Doyle, "The Adventure of the Six Napoleons," in *The Return of Sherlock Holmes* (Penguin Classics, 2008).

31. Sarah Netter, "Wash. Man Pulls off Robbery Using Craigslist, Pepper Spray," ABC News, October 1, 2008 (http://abcnews.go.com/US/story?id=5930862).

32. Jens Lund, with reply by István Deák, "The Legend of King Christian, an Exchange," *New York Review of Books* 30, no. 5 (1990) (http://www.nybooks.com/articles/

archives/1990/mar/29/the-legend-of-king-christian-an-exchange/). (That the specific case of the Yellow Star is fictional doesn't detract in any way from the Danes' heroic history of helping Jews hide and escape during the war.)

33. Leo Goldberger, ed., *The Rescue of the Danish Jews: Moral Courage Under Stress* (New York University Press, 1987).

34. Ben Kafka, *The Demon of Writing* (MIT Press, 2012), 67.

35. Jeremy Scahill and Glenn Greenwald, "The NSA's Secret Role in the U.S. Assassination Program," The Intercept, February 10, 2014 (https://firstlook.org/theintercept/2014/02/10/the-nsas-secret-role/).

36. Tor Project, "Frequently Asked Questions" (https://www.torproject.org/docs/faq.html.en#BetterAnonymity).

37. *State of California vs. Niroula*, Case INF 064492 (I.B. Cal.) (http://cryptome.org/2012/06/babble-tape.pdf).

38. Tim Jenkin, "Talking to Vula," *Mayibuye*, May–October 1995 (www.anc.org.za/show.php?id=4693).

CHAPTER 2

1. Ling Tseng and I.-Min Tso, "A Risky Defence by a Spider Using Conspicuous Decoys Resembling Itself in Appearance," *Animal Behavior* 78, no. 2 (2009): 425-431 (doi:10.1016/j.anbehav.2009.05.017).

2. Rip Empson, "Black Car Competitor Accuses Uber of DDoS-Style Attack; Uber Admits Tactics Are "Too Aggressive," TechCrunch, January 24, 2014 (http://techcrunch.com/2014/01/24/black-car-competitor-accuses-uber-of-shady-conduct-ddos-style-attack-uber-expresses-regret/).

3. "Le Gouvernement Veut Rendre les Avertisseurs de Radars Inefficaces," *Le Monde*, November 29, 2011 (http://www.lemonde.fr/societe/article/2011/11/29/les-avertisseurs-de-radars-seront-bientot-inefficaces_1610490_3224.html).

4. "Analysis of the "Flash Crash" Part 4, Quote Stuffing," Nanex, June 18, 2010 (http://www.nanex.net/20100506/FlashCrashAnalysis_Part4-1.html).

5. Ibid.

6. Joab Jackson, "Cards Games: Should Buyers Beware of How Supermarkets Use "Loyalty Cards" to Collect Personal Data?" *Baltimore City Paper*, October 1, 2003 (http://www.joabj.com/CityPaper/031001ShoppingCards.html).

7. Robert Ellis Smith, *Privacy Journal*, March 1999, p. 5.

8. http://epistolary.org/rob/bonuscard/, accessed October 25, 2010.

9. "The Ultimate Shopper," Cockeyed.com, last updated December 11, 2002 (http://www.cockeyed.com/pranks/safeway/ultimate_shopper.html).

10. "Hydra Project" (https://code.google.com/p/hydraproject/).

11. For a somewhat technical but accessible overview of BitTorrent that includes a lucid explanation of trackers, see Mikel Izal, Guillaume Urvoy-Keller, Ernst W. Biersack, Pascal Felber, Anwar Al Hamra, and Luis Garcés-Erice, "Dissecting BitTorrent: Five Months in a Torrent's Lifetime," *Passive and Active Network Measurement* 3015 (2004): 1–11 (doi: 10.1007/978-3-540-24668-8_1).

12. Hendrik Schulze and Klaus Mochalski, "Internet Study 2008/2009," Ipoque (http://www.christopher-parsons.com/Main/wp-content/uploads/2009/04/ipoque-internet-study-08-09.pdf).

13. Jacquelyn Burkell and Alexandre Fortier, "Privacy Policy Disclosures of Behavioural Tracking on Consumer Health Websites, *Proceedings of the American Society for Information Science and Technology* 50, no. 1 (May 2014): 1–9 (doi: 10.1002/meet.14505001087_.

14. Viola Ganter and Michael Strube, "Finding Hedges by Chasing Weasels: Hedge Detection Using Wikipedia Tags and Shallow Linguistic Features," in *Proceedings of the ACL-IJCNLP Conference Short Papers*, 2009 (http://dl.acm.org/citation.cfm?id=1667636).

15. David I. Holmes and Richard S. Forsyth, "The Federalist Revisited: New Directions in Authorship Attribution," *Literary and Linguistic Computing* 10, no. 2 (1995): 111–127 (doi: 10.1093/llc/10.2.111).

16. Josyula R. Rao and Pankaj Rohatgi, "Can Pseudonymity Really Guarantee Privacy?" in Proceedings of the 9th USENIX Security Symposium, 2000 (https://www.usenix.org/legacy/events/sec2000/full_papers/rao/rao_html/index.html).

17. Daniel Domscheit-Berg, *Inside WikiLeaks: My Time With Julian Assange at the World's Most Dangerous Website* (Crown, 2011).

18. Rao and Rohatgi, "Can Pseudonymity Really Guarantee Privacy?"

19. Moshe Koppel and Jonathan Schler, "Authorship Verification as a One-Class Classification Problem," in Proceedings of the 21st International Conference on Machine Learning, 2004 (doi: 10.1145/1015330.1015448).

20. On Anonymouth, see https://www.cs.drexel.edu/~pv42/thebiz/ and https://github.com/psal/anonymouth.

21. *Drive*, directed by Nicolas Winding Refn (Film District, 2011).

22. Mariano Ceccato, Massimiliano Di Penta, Jasvir Nagra, Paolo Falcarin, Filippo Ricca, Marco Torchiano, and Paolo Tonella, "The Effectiveness of Source Code Obfuscation: An Experimental Assessment," in Proceedings of 17th International Conference on Program Comprehension, 2009 (doi: 10.1109/ICPC.2009.5090041).

23. See Michael Mateas and Nick Monfort, "A Box, Darkly: Obfuscation, Weird Languages, and Code Aesthetics," in *Proceedings of the 6th Annual Digital Arts and Culture Conference*, 2005 (http://elmcip.net/node/3634).

24. Sanjam Garg, Craig Gentry, Shai Halevi, Mariana Raykova, Amit Sahai and Brent Waters, "Candidate Indistinguishability Obfuscation and Functional Encryption for all Circuits," in Proceedings of IEEE 54th Annual Symposium on Foundations of Computer Science, 2013 (doi: 10.1109/FOCS.2013.13).

25. Jeyavijayan Rajendran, Ozgur Sinanoglu, Michael Sam, and Ramesh Karri, "Security Analysis of Integrated Circuit Camouflaging," presented at ACM Conference on Computer and Communications Security, 2013 (doi: 10.1145/2508859.2516656).

26. From an interview with Ahearn: Joan Goodchild, "How to Disappear Completely," CSO, May 3, 2011 (http://www.csoonline.com/article/2128377/identity-theft-prevention/how-to-disappear-completely.html).

27. Stephen Carter, "United States Patent: 20070094738 A1—Techniques to Pollute Electronic Profiling," April 26, 2007 (http://www.google.com/patents/US20070094738).

28. Rachel Law, "Vortex" (http://www.milkred.net/vortex/). Much of the detail in this section is based on conversation with Law and on her presentation in the Tool Workshop Sessions at the Symposium on Obfuscation held at New York University in 2014.

29. Kevin Ludlow, "Bayesian Flooding and Facebook Manipulation," KevinLudlow. com, May 23, 2012 (http://www.kevinludlow.com/blog/1610/Bayesian_Flooding_and _Facebook_Manipulation_FB/).

30. Max Cho, "Unsell Yourself—A Protest Model Against Facebook," Yale Law & Technology, May 10, 2011 (http://www.yalelawtech.org/control-privacy-technology/ unsell-yourself-%E2%80%94-a-protest-model-against-facebook/).

31. Wanying Luo, Qi Xie, and Urs Hengartner, "FaceCloak: An Architecture for User Privacy on Social Networking Sites," in Proceedings of the 2009 IEEE International Conference on Privacy, Security, Risk and Trust (https://cs.uwaterloo.ca/~uhengart/ publications/passat09.pdf).

32. Charles Arthur, "How Low-Paid Workers at 'Click Farms' Create Appearance of Online Popularity," theguardian.com, August 2, 2013 (http://www.theguardian.com/ technology/2013/aug/02/click-farms-appearance-online-popularity).

33. Jaron Schneider, "Likes or Lies? How Perfectly Honest Business can be Overrun by Facebook Spammers," TheNextWeb, January 23, 2004 (http://thenextweb.com/ facebook/2014/01/23/likes-lies-perfectly-honest-businesses-can-overrun -facebook-spammers/).

34. Leo Selvaggio, "URME Surveillance," 2014 (http://www.urmesurveillance.com).

35. Francisco Goldman, *The Art of Political Murder: Who Killed the Bishop?* (Grove, 2008).

36. Ibid., 109.

CHAPTER 3

1. See the following for a brief look at the story of present-day privacy theory: Daniel J. Solove, *Understanding Privacy* (Harvard University Press, 2010); Ruth Gavison, "Privacy and the Limits of the Law," in *Philosophical Dimensions of Privacy: An Anthology*, ed. Ferdinand David Schoeman (Cambridge University Press, 1984); David Brin, *The Transparent Society* (Perseus Books, 1998); Priscilla M. Regan, *Legislating Privacy: Technology, Social Values and Public Policy* (University of North Carolina Press, 1995); Jeffrey H. Reiman, "Driving to the Panopticon: A Philosophical Exploration of the Risks to Privacy Posed by the Highway Technology of the Future," *Santa Clara High Technology Journal* 11, no. 1 (1995): 27–44 (http://digitalcommons.law.scu.edu/chtlj/vol11/ iss1/5); Alan F. Westin, "Science, Privacy and Freedom: Issues and Proposals for the

1970's. Part I—the Current Impact of Surveillance on Privacy," *Columbia Law Review* 66, no. 6 (1966): 1003–1050 (http://www.jstor.org/stable/1120997).

2. See the following for diverging theories: Helen Nissenbaum, *Privacy in Context: Technology, Policy and the Integrity of Social Life* (Stanford University Press, 2009); Julie E. Cohen, "Examined Lives: Informational Privacy and the Subject as Object," *Stanford Law Review* 52 (May 2000): 1373–1437 (http://scholarship.law.georgetown. edu/cgi/viewcontent.cgi?article=1819&context=facpub); Daniel J. Solove, "A Taxonomy of Privacy," *University of Pennsylvania Law Review* 154, no. 3 (2006): 477–560 (doi: 10.2307/40041279); Christena E. Nippert-Eng, *Islands of Privacy* (University of Chicago Press, 2010); Michael Birnhack and Yofi Tirosh, "Naked in Front of the Machine: Does Airport Scanning Violate Privacy?" *Ohio State Law Journal* 74, no. 6 (2013): 1263–1306.

3. See Paul Dourish, "Collective Information Practice: Exploring Privacy and Security as Social and Cultural Phenomena," *Human-Computer Interaction* 21, no. 3 (2006): 319–342 (doi: 10.1207/s15327051hci2103_2); Paul Dourish, Emily Troshynski, and Charlotte Lee, "Accountabilities of Presence: Reframing Location-Based Systems," in Proceedings of the SIGCHI Conference on Human Factors in Computing Systems, 2008 (doi: 10.1145/1357054.1357133).

4. Helen Nissenbaum, *Privacy in Context: Technology, Policy and the Integrity of Social Life* (Stanford University Press, 2009).

5. Kevin Kelly, *Out of Control: The New Biology of Machines, Social Systems and the Economic World* (Addison-Wesley, 1994) p. 176.

6. Gilbert Keith Chesterton, "The Sign of the Broken Sword," in *The Innocence of Father Brown* (Cassell, 1947) p. 143.

7. *Nichia Corp v. Argos Ltd.*, Case A3/2007/0572. EWCA Civ 741 (July 19, 2007) (http://www.bailii.org/ew/cases/EWCA/Civ/2007/741.html).

8. The Simpsons, "The Lemon of Troy," May 14, 1995.

9. Hanna Rose Shell, *Hide and Seek: Camouflage, Photography and the Media of Reconnaissance* (Zone Books, 2012).

10. Donald H. Rumsfeld, February 12, 2002 (11:30 a.m.), "DoD News Briefing—Secretary Rumsfeld and Gen. Myers," U.S. Department of Defense/Federal News Service, Inc. (http://www.defense.gov/transcripts/transcript.aspx?transcriptid=2636).

NOTES TO CHAPTER 3

11. Brad Templeton, "The Evils of Cloud Computing: Data Portability and Single Sign On," presented at BIL Conference, 2009 (http://www.vimeo.com/3946928).

12. Tal Zarsky, "Transparent Predictions," *University of Illinois Law Review* 2013, no. 4: 1519–1520.

13. Solon Barocas, "Data Mining and the Discourse on Discrimination," in Proceedings of Data Ethics Workshop at ACM Conference on Knowledge Discovery and Data Mining, New York, 2014.

14. See, in particular, Josh Lauer, "The Good Consumer: Credit Reporting and the Invention of Financial Identity in the United States, 1840–1940," *Enterprise & Society* 11, no. 4 (2010): 686–694 (doi: 10.1093/es/khq091); Lauer, *The Good Consumer: A History of Credit Surveillance and Financial Identity in America* (Columbia University Press, forthcoming).

15. Anthony Giddens, "Risk and Responsibility," *Modern Law Review* 62, no. 1 (1999): 1–10 (doi: 10.1111/1468-2230.00188). See also the elaboration of this idea in Ulrich Beck, *Risk Society: Toward a New Modernity* (SAGE, 1999).

16. Ben Cohen, "After Sandy, Wired New Yorkers Get Reconnected with Pay Phones," *Wall Street Journal*, October 31, 2012.

17. James C. Scott, *Weapons of the Weak: Everyday Forms of Peasant Resistance* (Yale University Press, 1987).

18. For a range of notable responses to surveillance, see the Gary T. Marx, "The Public as Partner? Technology Can Make Us Auxiliaries as Well as Vigilantes," *IEEE Security and Privacy* 11, no. 5 (2013): 56–61 (doi: http://doi.ieeecomputersociety.org/10.1109/MSP.2013.126); Marx, *Undercover: Police Surveillance in America* (University of California Press, 1989); Marx, "Technology and Social Control: The Search for the Illusive Silver Bullet Continues," in *International Encyclopedia of the Social and Behavioral Sciences*, second edition (Elsevier, forthcoming); Kenneth A. Bamberger and Deirdre K. Mulligan, "Privacy Decisionmaking in Administrative Agencies," *University of Chicago Law Review* 75, no. 1 (2008): 75–107 (http://ssrn.com/abstract=1104728); Katherine J. Strandburg and Daniela Stan Raicu, *Privacy and Technologies of Identity: A Cross-Disciplinary Conversation* (Springer, 2006).

19. Scott elaborates on this concept in depth in *Domination and the Arts of Resistance: Hidden Transcripts* (Yale University Press, 1992).

20. For arguments regarding the development of the idea of the "monetization" of data and the role it plays in present-day businesses and institutions, see Gina Neff, "Why Big Data Won't Cure Us," *Big Data* 1, no. 3 (2013): 117–123 (doi: 10.1089/big.2013.0029); Brittany Fiore-Silfvast and Gina Neff, "Communication, Mediation, and the Expectations of Data: Data Valences across Health and Wellness Communities," unpublished manuscript (under review at *International Journal of Communication*).

21. Google Inc., Securities Exchange Commission Form 10-Q for the period ending October 31, 2009 (filed November 4, 2009), p. 23, from SEC.gov (http://www.sec.gov/Archives/edgar/data/1288776/000119312509222384/d10q.htm).

22. Martin Heidegger, *The Question Concerning Technology and Other Essays* (Garland, 1977).

23. For more on Snowden, see Glenn Greenwald, Ewen MacAskill, and Laura Poitras, "Edward Snowden: The Whistleblower Behind the NSA Surveillance Revelations," theguardian.com, June 11, 2013 (http://www.theguardian.com/world/2013/jun/09/edward-snowden-nsa-whistleblower-surveillance); Ladar Levison, "Secrets, Lies and Snowden's Email: Why I Was Forced to Shut Down Lavabit," theguardian.com, May 20, 2014 (http://www.theguardian.com/commentisfree/2014/may/20/why-did-lavabit-shut-down-snowden-email); Glenn Greenwald, *No Place to Hide: Edward Snowden, the NSA and the U.S. Surveillance State* (Metropolitan Books, 2014); Katherine J. Strandburg, "Home, Home on the Web and Other Fourth Amendment Implications of Technosocial Change," *University of Maryland Law Review* 70, April 2011: 614–680 (http://ssrn.com/abstract=1808071).

24. The idea of "kleptography," in its more expanded definition, is a useful way of understanding this approach. For the initial, narrower definition—the use of black-box cryptosystems implemented on closed hardware—see Adam Young and Moti Yung, "Kleptography: Using Cryptography Against Cryptography," in *Advances in Cryptology—Eurocrypt '97*, ed. Walter Fumy (Springer, 1997). For the more expansive definition—persuading your adversary to use a form of cryptography you know you can break, or using inferior alternatives for reasons of availability or convenience—see Philip Hallam-Baker, "PRISM-Proof Security Considerations," Internet Engineering Task Force (IETF) draft 3.4, 2013 (https://tools.ietf.org/html/draft-hallambaker-prismproof-req-00#section-3.4).

25. Arvid Narayanan, "What Happened to the Crypto Dream? Part 2," *IEEE Security and Privacy* 11, no. 3 (2013): 68–71 (doi: http://doi.ieeecomputersociety.org/10.1109/MSP.2013.75).

CHAPTER 4

1. On TrackMeNot, see http://cs.nyu.edu/trackmenot/.

2. Gary T. Marx, "A Tack in the Shoe: Neutralizing and Resisting New Surveillance," *Journal of Social Issues* 59, no. 2 (2003): 369–390 (doi: 10.1111/1540-4560.00069).

3. See James Edwin Mahon, "The Definition of Lying and Deception," in *The Stanford Encyclopedia of Philosophy* (http://plato.stanford.edu/archives/fall2008/entries/lying-definition/); John Finnis, "Aquinas' Moral, Political and Legal Philosophy," in *The Stanford Encyclopedia of Philosophy* (http://plato.stanford.edu/archives/sum2014/entries/aquinas-moral-political/).

4. Sissela Bok, *Lying: Moral Choice in Public and Private Life* (Vintage Books, 1999).

5. Joseph T. Meyerowitz and Romit Roy Choudhury, CacheCloack, 2009 (http://www.cachecloak.co.uk/).

6. See also Chris Jay Hoofnagle, Ashkan Soltani, Nathaniel Good, and Dietrich J. Wambach, "Behavioral Advertising: The Offer You Can't Refuse," *Harvard Law & Policy Review* 6, August (2012): 273–296 (http://ssrn.com/abstract=2137601); Aleecia M. McDonald and Lorrie F. Cranor, "The Cost of Reading Privacy Policies," *I/S* 4, no. 3 (2008): 540–565 (http://lorrie.cranor.org/pubs/readingPolicyCost-authorDraft.pdf); Katherine J. Strandburg, "Free Fall: The Online Market's Consumer Preference Disconnect," *University of Chicago Legal Forum* 95 (2013): 95–172 (http://ssrn.com/abstract=2323961); Chris Jay Hoofnagle and Jan Whittington, "Free: Accounting for the Costs of the Internet's Most Popular Price," *UCLA Law Review* 61 (2014): 606–670 (http://ssrn.com/abstract=2235962).

7. See Joseph Turow, Chris Jay Hoofnagle, Dierdre K. Mulligan, Nathaniel Good, and Jens Grossklags, "The Federal Trade Commission and Consumer Privacy in the Coming Decade," *I/S* 3, no. 3 (2007): 723–749 (http://ssrn.com/abstract=2365578); Joseph Turow, *The Daily You: How the New Advertising Industry Is Defining Your Identity and Your Worth* (Yale University Press, 2013).

8. Isaiah Berlin, *The Crooked Timber of Humanity: Chapters in the History of Ideas* (Princeton University Press, 2013), 2.

9. Daniel J. Solove and Paul M. Schwartz, *Privacy Law Fundamentals*, second edition (International Association of Privacy Professionals, 2013).

10. See Daniel J. Solove, "Privacy Self-Management and the Consent Dilemma," *Harvard Law Review* 126 (2013): 1880–1903 (http://ssrn.com/abstract=2171018); Lauren E. Willis, "Why Not Privacy by Default?" *Berkeley Technology Law Journal* 29 (2014): 61–134 (http://ssrn.com/abstract=2349766); James Grimmelman, "The Sabotage of Do Not Track," The Laboratorium, June 19, 2012 (http://laboratorium.net/archive/2012/06/19/the_sabotage_of_do_not_track).

11. For more on Snowden, see Glenn Greenwald, Ewen MacAskill, and Laura Poitras, "Edward Snowden: The Whistleblower Behind the NSA Surveillance Revelations," theguardian.com, June 11, 2013 (http://www.theguardian.com/world/2013/jun/09/edward-snowden-nsa-whistleblower-surveillance); Ladar Levison, "Secrets, Lies and Snowden's Email: Why I Was Forced to Shut Down Lavabit," theguardian.com, May 20, 2014 (http://www.theguardian.com/commentisfree/2014/may/20/why-did-lavabit-shut-down-snowden-email); Glenn Greenwald, *No Place to Hide: Edward Snowden, the NSA and the U.S. Surveillance State* (Metropolitan Books, 2014); Joshua Eaton and Ben Piven, "Timeline of the Edward Snowden Revelations, theguardian.com, June 5, 2013 (http://america.aljazeera.com/articles/multimedia/timeline-edward-snowden-revelations.html).

12. John Rawls, *A Theory of Justice* (Harvard University Press, 1971).

13. Ibid., 173.

14. Arthur Ripstein, *Equality, Responsibility and the Law* (Cambridge University Press, 1999).

15. Jeroen Van Den Hoven and Emma Rooksby, "Distributive Justice and the Value of Information: A (Broadly) Rawlsian Approach," in *Information Technology and Moral Philosophy*, ed. John Weckert (Cambridge University Press, 2008), 376.

16. See danah boyd, *It's Complicated: The Social Lives of Networked Teens* (Yale University Press, 2014); Colin Koopman, "Internetworked Publics: The Emerging Political Conditions of the Internet," paper presented at Ars Synthetica: The Anthropology of the Contemporary, Santa Cruz, 2009.

17. Francisco Goldman, *The Art of Political Murder: Who Killed the Bishop?* (Grove, 2007).

18. Anatole France, *The Red Lily* (Borgo, 2002), 64.

19. Philip Pettit, *Republicanism: A Theory of Freedom and Government* (Oxford University Press, 1997), 73, 79.

20. See Viktor Mayer-Schönberger and Kenneth Cukier, *Big Data: A Revolution That Will Transform How We Live, Work and Think* (Houghton Mifflin Harcourt, 2013), 94; Solon Barocas, "Data Mining and the Discourse on Discrimination," in Proceedings of Data Ethics Workshop at Conference on Knowledge Discovery and Data Mining, 2014; Tal Zarsky, "Transparent Predictions," *University of Illinois Law Review* 2013, no. 4 (2013): 1519–1520.

21. Pettit, *Republicanism*, 80, 272.

22. Rawls, *A Theory of Justice*.

23. Mayer-Schönberger and Cukier, *Big Data*; Turow, *The Daily You*.

24. Jeremy Waldron, *Torture, Terror and Trade-Offs: Philosophy for the White House* (Oxford University Press, 2012).

25. Turow, *The Daily You*; Hoofnagle, Soltani, Good, and Wambach, "Behavioral Advertising."

CHAPTER 5

1. *Get Smart*, "Mr. Big," September 18, 1965.

2. See Cynthia Dwork and Aaron Roth, "The Algorithmic Foundations of Differential Privacy," *Foundations and Trends in Theoretical Computer Science* 9, no. 3–4 (2014): 211–407 (doi: http://dx.doi.org/10.1561/0400000042); Cynthia Dwork, Frank McSherry, Kobbi Nissim, and Adam Smith, "Calibrating Noise to Sensitivity in Private Data Analysis," in Proceedings of the Third Conference on Theory of Cryptography, 2006 (doi: 10.1007/11681878_14).

3. Adam Shostack, *Threat Modeling: Designing for Security* (Wiley, 2014).

4. danah boyd, *It's Complicated: The Social Lives of Networked Teens* (Yale University Press, 2014), 65.

5. Ibid., 69.

6. Gion Green, "Rating Files, Safes, and Vaults," in *Handbook of Loss Prevention and Crime Prevention*, ed. Lawrence Fennelly (Elsevier, 2012), 358.

BIBLIOGRAPHY

Bamberger, Kenneth A., and Deirdre K. Mulligan. "Privacy Decisionmaking in Administrative Agencies." *University of Chicago Law Review* 75, no. 1 (2008): 75–107 (http://ssrn.com/abstract=1104728).

Barbaro, Michael, and Tom Zeller Jr. "A Face Is Exposed for AOL Searcher No. 4417749." *New York Times*, August 9, 2006.

Barocas, Solon. "Data Mining and the Discourse on Discrimination." In Proceedings of Data Ethics Workshop at ACM Conference on Knowledge Discovery and Data Mining, New York, 2014.

Beck, Ulrich. *Risk Society: Towards a New Modernity*. London: SAGE, 1999.

Berlin, Isaiah. *The Crooked Timber of Humanity: Chapters in the History of Ideas*. Princeton University Press, 2013.

Birnhack, Michael, and Yofi Tirosh. "Naked in Front of the Machine: Does Airport Scanning Violate Privacy?" *Ohio State Law Journal* 74, no. 6 (2013): 1263–1306 (http://ssrn.com/abstract=2234476).

Bok, Sissela. *Lying: Moral Choice in Public and Private Life*. New York: Vintage Books, 1999.

boyd, danah. *It's Complicated: The Social Lives of Networked Teens*. New Haven: Yale University Press, 2014.

Brin, David. *The Transparent Society*. New York: Perseus Books, 1998.

Burkell, Jacquelyn, and Alexandre Fortier. "Privacy Policy Disclosures of Behavioural Tracking on Consumer Health Websites." *Proceedings of the American Society for Information Science and Technology* 50, no. 1 (2014): 1–9 (doi:10.1002/meet.14505001087).

Ceccato, Mariano, Massimiliano Di Penta, Jasvir Nagra, Paolo Falcarin, Filippo Ricca, Marco Torchiano, and Paolo Tonella. "The Effectiveness of Source Code Obfuscation: An Experimental Asessment." In Proceedings of 17th International Conference on Program Comprehension, 2009 (doi: 10.1109/ICPC.2009.5090041).

Chesterton, Gilbert Keith. "The Sign of the Broken Sword." In *The Innocence of Father Brown*. London: Cassell, 1947.

Cho, Max. "Unsell Yourself—A Protest Model Against Facebook." Yale Law & Technology blog May 10, 2011 (http://www.yalelawtech.org/control-privacy-technology/unsell-yourself-%E2%80%94-a-protest-model-against-facebook/).

Cohen, Fred. "The Use of Deception Techniques: Honeypots and Decoys." In *Handbook of Information Security*, volume 3, ed. Hossein Bidgoli. Hoboken: Wiley, 2006.

Cohen, Julie E. "Examined Lives: Informational Privacy and the Subject as Object." *Stanford Law Review* 52, May (2000): 1373–1437 (http://scholarship.law.georgetown.edu/cgi/viewcontent.cgi?article=1819&context=facpub).

Deseriis, Marco. "Lots of Money Because I Am Many: The Luther Blissett Project and the Multiple-Use Name Strategy." Thamyris/Intersecting 21 (2011): 65–93.

Domscheit-Berg, Daniel. *Inside WikiLeaks: My Time with Julian Assange at the World's Most Dangerous Website*. New York: Crown, 2011.

Dourish, Paul, Emily Troshynski, and Charlotte Lee. "Accountabilities of Presence: Reframing Location-Based Systems." In Proceedings of the SIGCHI Conference on Human Factors in Computing Systems, 2008 (doi: 10.1145/1357054.1357133).

Dourish, Paul. "Collective Information Practice: Exploring Privacy and Security as Social and Cultural Phenomena." *Human-Computer Interaction* 21, no. 3 (2006): 319–342 (doi:10.1207/s15327051hci2103_2).

Dwork, Cynthia, and Aaron Roth. "The Algorithmic Foundations of Differential Privacy." *Foundations and Trends in Theoretical Computer Science* 9, no. 3–4 (2014): 211–407 (doi: 10.1561/0400000042).

Dwork, Cynthia, Frank McSherry, Kobbi Nissim, and Adam Smith. "Calibrating Noise to Sensitivity in Private Data Analysis." In Proceedings of the Third Conference on Theory of Cryptography, 2006 (doi: 10.1007/11681878_14).

Finkel, Meir. *On Flexibility: Recovery from Technological and Doctrinal Surprise on the Battlefield*. Stanford University Press, 2011.

Finnis, John. "Aquinas' Moral, Political and Legal Philosophy." In *The Stanford Encyclopedia of Philosophy*, ed. Edward N. Zalta (http://plato.stanford.edu/archives/sum2014/entries/aquinas-moral-political/).

Fiore-Silfvast, Brittany and Gina Neff. "Communication, Mediation, and the Expectations of Data: Data Valences across Health and Wellness Communities." Under review at *International Journal of Communication*.

France, Anatole. *The Red Lily*. San Bernardino: Borgo, 2002.

Ganter, Viola, and Michael Strube. "Finding Hedges by Chasing Weasels: Hedge Detection Using Wikipedia Tags and Shallow Linguistic Features." In *Proceedings of the ACL-IJCNLP Conference Short Papers*, 2009 (http://dl.acm.org/citation.cfm?id=1667636).

Garg, Sanjam, Craig Gentry, Shai Halevi, Mariana Raykova, Amit Sahai, and Brent Waters. "Candidate Indistinguishability Obfuscation and Functional Encryption for all Circuits." Presented at IEEE 54th Annual Symposium on Foundations of Computer Science, 2013 (doi: 10.1109/FOCS.2013.13).

Gavison, Ruth. "Privacy and the Limits of the Law." In *Philosophical Dimensions of Privacy: An Anthology*, ed. Ferdinand David Schoeman. Cambridge University Press, 1984.

Giddens, Anthony. "Risk and Responsibility." *Modern Law Review* 62, no. 1 (1999): 1–10 (doi:10.1111/1468-2230.00188).

Goldberger, Leo, ed. *The Rescue of the Danish Jews: Moral Courage Under Stress*. New York University Press, 1987.

Goldman, Francisco. *The Art of Political Murder: Who Killed the Bishop?* New York: Grove, 2007.

Green, Gion. "Rating Files, Safes, and Vaults." In *Handbook of Loss Prevention and Crime Prevention*, ed. Lawrence Fennelly. Oxford: Elsevier, 2012.

Greenberg, Andy. *This Machine Kills Secrets: How WikiLeakers, Cypherpunks, and Hacktivists Aim to Free the World's Information*. New York: Dutton, 2012.

Greenwald, Glenn. *No Place to Hide: Edward Snowden, the NSA and the U.S. Surveillance State*. New York: Metropolitan Books, 2014.

Habinek, Thomas. *The World of Roman Song: From Ritualized Speech to Social Order*. Baltimore: Johns Hopkins University Press, 2005.

Heidegger, Martin. *The Question Concerning Technology and Other Essays*. New York: Garland, 1977.

Hellmuth, Phil Marvin Karlins, and Joe Navarro. *Phil Hellmuth Presents Read 'Em and Reap*. New York: HarperCollins, 2006.

Holmes, David I., and Richard S. Forsyth. "The Federalist Revisited: New Directions in Authorship Attribution." *Literary and Linguistic Computing* 10, no. 2 (1995): 111–127 (doi: 10.1093/llc/10.2.111).

Hoofnagle, Chris Jay, and Jan Whittington. "Free: Accounting for the Costs of the Internet's Most Popular Price." *UCLA Law Review. University of California, Los Angeles. School of Law* 61 (2014): 606–670 (http://ssrn.com/abstract=2235962).

Hoofnagle, Chris Jay, Ashkan Soltani, Nathaniel Good, and Dietrich J. Wambach. "Behavioral Advertising: The Offer You Can't Refuse." *Harvard Law & Policy Review* 6, August (2012): 273–296 (http://ssrn.com/abstract=2137601).

Howe, Daniel, and Helen Nissenbaum. "TrackMeNot: Resisting Surveillance in Web Search." In *Lessons From the Identity Trail: Anonymity, Privacy and Identity in a Networked Society*, ed. Ian Kerr, Carole Luckock, and Valerie Steeves. Oxford University Press, 2009.

Izal, Mikel, Guillaume Urvoy-Keller, Ernst W. Biersack, Pascal Felber, Anwar Al Hamra, and Luis Garcés-Erice. "Dissecting BitTorrent: Five Months in a Torrent's Lifetime." In *Passive and Active Network Measurement*, ed. Chadi Barakat and Ian Pratt. Berlin: Springer, 2004..

Jenkin, Tim. "Talking to Vula." *Mayibuye*, May–October 1995 (www.anc.org.za/show.php?id=4693).

Kafka, Ben. *The Demon of Writing*. Cambridge: MIT Press, 2012.

Kelly, Kevin. *Out of Control: The New Biology of Machines, Social Systems and the Economic World*. Indianapolis: Addison-Wesley, 1994.

Koopman, Colin. "Internetworked Publics: The Emerging Political Conditions of the Internet." Paper presented at Ars Synthetica: The Anthropology of the Contemporary, Santa Cruz, 2009.

Koppel, Moshe, and Jonathan Schler. "Authorship Verification as a One-Class Classification Problem." In Proceedings of the 21st International Conference on Machine Learning, 2004 (doi: 10.1145/1015330.1015448).

Lane, Julia, Victoria Stodden, Stefan Bender, and Helen Nissenbaum, eds. *Privacy, Big Data, and the Public Good: Frameworks for Engagement*. Cambridge University Press, 2014.

Lauer, Josh. "The Good Consumer: Credit Reporting and the Invention of Financial Identity in the United States, 1840–1940." *Enterprise and Society* 11, no. 4 (2010): 686–694 (doi:10.1093/es/khq091).

Lauer, Josh. *The Good Consumer: A History of Credit Surveillance and Financial Identity in America*. New York: Columbia University Press, forthcoming.

Lund, Jens, with reply by István Deák. "The Legend of King Christian: An Exchange." *New York Review of Books* 30, no. 5 (1990) (http://www.nybooks.com/articles/archives/1990/mar/29/the-legend-of-king-christian-an-exchange/).

Luo, Wanying, Qi Xie, and Urs Hengartner. "FaceCloak: An Architecture for User Privacy on Social Networking Sites." In Proceedings of the 2009 IEEE International Conference on Privacy, Security, Risk and Trust (https://cs.uwaterloo.ca/~uhengart/publications/passat09.pdf).

Mahon, James Edwin. "The Definition of Lying and Deception." In *The Stanford Encyclopedia of Philosophy*, ed. Edward N. Zalta (http://plato.stanford.edu/archives/fall2008/entries/lying-definition/).

Marx, Gary T. "A Tack in the Shoe: Neutralizing and Resisting New Surveillance." *Journal of Social Issues* 59, no. 2 (2003): 369–390 (doi:10.1111/1540-4560.00069).

Marx, Gary T. "Technology and Social Control: The Search for the Illusive Silver Bullet Continues." In *International Encyclopedia of the Social and Behavioral Sciences*, second edition. Oxford: Elsevier, forthcoming.

Marx, Gary T. "The Public as Partner? Technology Can Make Us Auxiliaries as Well as Vigilantes." *IEEE Security and Privacy* 11, no. 5 (2013): 56–61 (doi: http://DOI.ieeecomputersociety.org/10.1109/MSP.2013.126).

Marx, Gary T. *Undercover: Police Surveillance in America*. Oakland: University of California Press, 1989.

Maslinsky, Kirill, Sergey Koltcov, and Olessia Koltslova. "Changes in the Topical Structure of Russian-Language LiveJournal: The Impact of Elections 2011." Research Paper WP BPR 14/SOC/2013, National Research University, Moscow, 2013.

Mateas, Michael, and Nick Monfort. "A Box, Darkly: Obfuscation, Weird Languages, and Code Aesthetics." In Proceedings of the 6th Annual Digital Arts and Culture Conference, 2005 (http://elmcip.net/node/3634).

Mayer-Schönberger, Viktor, and Kennth Cukier. *Big Data: A Revolution That Will Transform How We Live, Work and Think*. New York: Houghton Mifflin Harcourt, 2013.

McDonald, Aleecia M., and Lorrie F. Cranor. "The Cost of Reading Privacy Policies." *I/S* 4, no. 3 (2008): 540–565 (http://lorrie.cranor.org/pubs/readingPolicyCost-authorDraft.pdf).

Meyerowitz, Joseph, and Romit R. Choudhury. "Hiding Stars with Fireworks: Location Privacy through Camouflage." In Proceedings of the 15th Annual International Conference on Mobile Computing and Networking. 2009.

Moore, Alan, and David Lloyd. *V for Vendetta*. New York: Vertigo/DC Comics, 1982.

Narayanan, Arvid. "What Happened to the Crypto Dream? Part 2." *IEEE Security and Privacy* 11, no. 3 (2013): 68–71 (doi: http://DOI.ieeecomputersociety.org/10.1109/MSP.2013.75),

Neff, Gina. "Why Big Data Won't Cure Us." *Big Data* 1, no. 3 (2013): 117–123 (doi:10.1089/big.2013.0029).

Nippert-Eng, Christena E. *Islands of Privacy*. University of Chicago Press, 2010.

Nissenbaum, Helen. *Privacy in Context: Technology, Policy and the Integrity of Social Life*. Stanford University Press, 2009.

Orcutt, Mike. "Twitter Mischief Plagues Mexico's Election." *MIT Technology Review*, June 21, 2014 (http://www.technologyreview.com/news/428286/twitter-mischief -plagues-mexicos-election/).

Parkhomenko, Ekaterina, and Arch Tait. "Blog Talk." *Index on Censorship* 37, February (2008): 174–178 (doi: 10.1080/03064220701882822).

Pettit, Philip. *Republicanism: A Theory of Freedom and Government*. Oxford University Press, 1997.

Rajendran, Jeyavijayan, Ozgur Sinanoglu, Michael Sam, and Ramesh Karri. "Security Analysis of Integrated Circuit Camouflaging." Presented at ACM Conference on Computer and Communications Security, 2013 (doi:10.1145/2508859.2516656).

Rao, Josyula R., and Pankaj Rohatgi. "Can Pseudonymity Really Guarantee Privacy?" In Proceedings of the 9th USENIX Security Symposium, 2000 (https://www.usenix.org/legacy/events/sec2000/full_papers/rao/rao_html/index.html).

Rawls, John. *A Theory of Justice*. Cambridge: Harvard University Press, 1971.

Regan, Priscilla M. *Legislating Privacy: Technology, Social Values and Public Policy*. Chapel Hill: University of North Carolina Press, 1995.

Reiman, Jeffrey H. "Driving to the Panopticon: A Philosophical Exploration of the Risks to Privacy Posed by the Highway Technology of the Future." *Santa Clara High Technology Journal* 11, no. 1 (1995): 27–44 (http://digitalcommons.law.scu.edu/chtlj/vol11/iss1/5).

Ripstein. Arthur. *Equality, Responsibility and the Law*. Cambridge University Press, 1999.

Scott, James C. *Domination and the Arts of Resistance: Hidden Transcripts*. New Haven: Yale University Press, 1992.

Shell, Hanna Rose. *Hide and Seek: Camouflage, Photography, and the Media of Reconnaissance*. Cambridge: Zone Books, 2012.

Shostack, Adam. *Threat Modeling: Designing for Security*. Indianapolis: Wiley, 2014.

Solove, Daniel J. "A Taxonomy of Privacy." *University of Pennsylvania Law Review* 154, no. 3 (2006): 477–560 (doi: 10.2307/40041279).

Solove, Daniel J. "Privacy Self-Management and the Consent Dilemma." *Harvard Law Review* 126 (2013): 1880–1903. http://ssrn.com/abstract=2171018.

Solove, Daniel J. *Understanding Privacy*. Cambridge: Harvard University Press, 2010.

Solove, Daniel J., and Paul M. Schwartz. *Privacy Law Fundamentals*, second edition. Portsmouth: International Association of Privacy Professionals, 2013.

Strandburg, Katherine J. "Free Fall: The Online Market's Consumer Preference Disconnect." *University of Chicago Legal Forum* 95 (2013): 95–172. http://ssrn.com/abstract=2323961.

Strandburg, Katherine J. "Home, Home on the Web and Other Fourth Amendment Implications of Technosocial Change." *University of Maryland Law Review* 70, April (2011): 614–680 (http://ssrn.com/abstract=1808071)>

Strandburg, Katherine J., and Daniela Stan Raicu. *Privacy and Technologies of Identity: A Cross-Disciplinary Conversation*. New York: Springer, 2006.

Templeton, Brad. "The Evils of Cloud Computing: Data Portability and Single Sign On." Presented at BIL Conference, 2009 (http://www.vimeo.com/3946928).

Toubiana, Vincent, and Helen Nissenbaum. "An Analysis of Google Logs Retention Policies." *Journal of Privacy and Confidentiality* 3, no. 1 (2011): 3–26. http://repository.cmu.edu/jpc/vol3/iss1/2/.

Tseng, Ling, and I.-Min Tso. "A Risky Defense by a Spider Using Conspicuous Decoys Resembling Itself in Appearance." *Animal Behaviour* 78, no. 2 (2009): 425–431 (doi: 10.1016/j.anbehav.2009.05.017).

Turow, Joseph. *The Daily You: How the New Advertising Industry is Defining Your Identity and Your Worth*. New Haven: Yale University Press, 2013.

Turow, Joseph, Chris Jay Hoofnagle, Dierdre K. Mulligan, Nathaniel Good, and Jens Grossklags. "The Federal Trade Commission and Consumer Privacy in the Coming Decade." *I/S* 3, no. 3 (2007): 723–749 (http://ssrn.com/abstract=2365578).

van den Hoven, Jeroen, and Emma Rooksby. "Distributive Justice and the Value of Information: A (Broadly) Rawlsian Approach." In *Information Technology and Moral Philosophy*, ed. John Wecker. Cambridge University Press, 2008.

Waldron, Jeremy. *Torture, Terror and Trade-Offs: Philosophy for the White House*. Oxford University Press, 2012.

Westin, Alan F. "Science, Privacy and Freedom: Issues and Proposals for the 1970's. Part I—the Current Impact of Surveillance on Privacy." *Columbia Law Review* 66, no. 6 (1966): 1003–1050 (http://www.jstor.org/stable/1120997).

Willis, Lauren E. "Why Not Privacy by Default?" *Berkeley Technology Law Journal* 29 (2014): 61–134 (http://ssrn.com/abstract=2349766).

Young, Adam, and Moti Yung. "Kleptography: Using Cryptography Against Cryptography." In *Advances in Cryptology—Eurocrypt '97*, ed. Walter Fumy, 62–74. Berlin: Springer, 1997.

Zarsky, Tal. "Transparent Predictions." *University of Illinois Law Review* 2013, no. 4: 1519–1520.

INDEX

Hidden transcript, 56–58
High-frequency trading (HFT), 27, 28
Human analysis limitation, 33–35

Identical confederates and objects, 16, 17
Identity prosthetics, 40, 41
Imitation attacks, 32
Imitations, 9–12
Implementation questions, 84–90
Information asymmetry, 48–53

Jenkin, Tim, 22–24
Justice, 74–80, 83
Justification, 63, 64

Likefarming, 40
Linguistic constructions, 30, 31
LiveJournal, 9–10, 9–12
Location-based services (LBSs), 12, 13
Loyalty card swapping, 28, 29
Ludlow, Kevin, 38, 39
Lying, 64, 65

Marx, Gary, 56, 63
Masks, 40, 41
Means v. ends, 70–83
Medical information, 31, 93–95
Mexican political struggle, 11, 12
Misleading signals, 8, 9
Morality, 70–83
Moral responsibility, 68, 69

National Security Agency (NSA), 18, 19
Necessary visibility, 85, 86
Network effect, 90, 91

Obfuscation attacks, 32, 33
OpenLeaks, 14, 15
Operation Vula, 21–24, 88, 89
Opting out, 53–58

Overproduction of documents, 17, 18
Oversupply, 17, 18

Patterns, 7, 15
Personal disinformation, 35
Plausible deniability, 14
Political questions, 71, 75–78, 83
Political uses, 9–12, 90
Pollution, 69, 70, 77
Power, 9–12, 48–53, 55–58, 78–80
Predictive software, 51
Press, Ronnie, 24
Privacy, 45–48, 50, 58, 61, 62, 72–76, 87–89
Privacy systems, 58–62
Profiling interference, 90
Protest expression, 90

Quote stuffing, 27, 28

Radar, 7, 8, 26, 88
Rawls, John, 76–78
Resource limitations, 65–67
Robots, 50
Rob's Giant Bonus Card Swap Meet, 29
Russian political struggle, 9–11

Scott, James C., 55–57
Selective obfuscation, 92–94
Selvaggio, Leo, 40, 41
Service denial, 9–12
Shopping pattern tracking, 28, 29
Shuffling SIM cards, 18, 19
Social benefits, 80–82
Social media, 86
Social stenography, 86
South African political struggle, 21–24
Stand-ins, 25
Stock exchanges, 27, 28
Stylometric analysis attacks, 31–33
Subversion, 69, 70
System damage, 69, 70